With her fat[her]

The Diary of a
Victorian Rector's Daughter

Stephen Huggins

Stephen Huggins

St Nicholas' Church

Copyright © 2019 Stephen Huggins

All rights reserved.

ISBN: 9781798738740

With her father's love

DEDICATION

To Mabel, Ruth and all daughters of the clergy.

Who can find a virtuous woman? for her price is far above rubies.
Proverbs 31: 10

Stephen Huggins

CONTENTS

Forward 1
Acknowledgements 2
An Introduction 3
Notes 12
January 14
February 21
March 28
April 37
May 45
June 54
July 63
August 73
September 83
October 92
November 102
December 111
Notes 119
About the Author 132

FORWARD

On her death in 1950 Mabel Ridout left no children to whom she could bequeath her life effects. In all probability, the many volumes of her diary, together with everything else, will simply have been disposed of as often goes on in these situations. The diary for 1887 came into my possession a few years ago and I know that there are others in existence.

It is a privilege to read the diary of another person for the writer will have had no possible inclination that what was written, both of themselves and others, would eventually become public. Perhaps it is this that makes the diary as a genre so valuable as historical evidence.

In this diary may be seen a way of life in rural England towards the end of the 19th Century. Moreover, it provides insight to the life experience of a very well defined group – the daughters of the Anglican clergy. There were notable diarists among the Victorian clergy but not so very many published diaries which had been kept by their daughters. Here is the life of one such daughter, Mabel Ridout, as she recorded it in 1887.

Stephen Huggins

ACKNOWLEDGEMENTS

I should like to thank the Cadbury Research Library: Special Collections, University of Birmingham (www.birmingham.ac.uk/facilities/cadbury)

and

the Church Missions Society (www.churchmissionsociety.org/church-mission-society-archives) for their kind permission to use the pictures of Mabel and Sidney Smith.

My thanks again to Lolly for all her invaluable help with this book.

With her father's love

Mabel Ridout and her diary for 1887

An Introduction

Mabel Ridout

Mabel Katharine Ridout was born in the Rectory of St Nicholas, Sandhurst[1] in Kent on 19th October 1866. Her parents were George Ridout and Sophia, nee Daniell[2].

St Nicholas' Rectory, which stood close to the church, was a large and imposing dwelling probably of 18th Century or earlier origins, being extended in the 19th

St Nicholas' Rectory

Century. It was constructed of red brick with some tile hanging to the gables, tiled roof and brick chimney stacks.

In 1887 the Rectory had already been home to the large Ridout family for some 30 years[3] and there were also servants but by that year it would seem that only Mabel and one sister were still living at home[4].

Life in the Rectory appears to have been both busy and well ordered. In addition to those who called at the house for the Rector's ministerial attention there were frequent other visitors both for her parents, George and Sophia, as well as Mabel and her siblings.

There is no suggestion from Mabel's diary that relationships within the family were anything less than loving and mutually supportive. They read to one another, sang together, went for country walks and horse riding together and played a variety of board games in the long evenings.

Mabel's diary does provide a useful insight into her life, character and Christian faith. She was a practical young woman making clothes for both herself and others. Mabel took an interest in the plants, shrubs and trees of the rectory garden, knew the Latin names of plants and would attend local flower shows. She helped to keep bees and collected their honey, made jam from locally picked fruit and put her hand to the production of cough mixture. Mabel was a keen reader both for pleasure and also study which included French, German, Greek and Algebra. Photography was an interest. The countryside and nature were a delight to her as were its associated pursuits including

With her father's love

horse riding and going ferreting with her brothers. Mabel was a very keen letter writer through which a wide network of friends was kept in touch as well as being a committed diarist for she kept them for many years other than 1887.

It is also possible to make some tentative observations about Mabel's character from the evidence of the diary. Mabel was fortunate to have many friends and a wide circle of other social contacts deriving from her position as the Rector's daughter. Yet there is not one occasion in the diary when any critical, judgemental or unkind word is made of anybody. What makes this particularly significant is that it is precisely in a diary, perhaps, where the individual might feel most able to record such thoughts and feelings.

A further feature which emerges is how at ease Mabel appears to be both with herself and the circumstances of her life. As a child born in the Rectory Mabel was socially and economically privileged in relation to the vast majority of the villagers that is clear, of course. At the same time there is no evidence in the diary of this young woman, with her sense of vocation and general level of education, feeling confined by the limitations of a life spent, year upon year, in a small rural parish in Kent. Indeed, it may be seen that Mabel took her circumstances and worked with them to their full potential. The diary shows her as a regular visitor to many homes in the parish often taking people soup or clothes and reading to them. While this may be seen as an extension to and support for her father's pastoral ministry it also had an integrity, momentum and purpose of its own. Mabel seemed to understand the reciprocity of enrichment which comes about being involved in the lives of others. A further example of the way in which Mabel made the best of her circumstances is that she takes a simple interest in what is going on around her. She goes to see some new born calves and a lamb, finds the appearance of a traction engine worthy of note and delights in nature and the changing of the seasons. There is no hint whatsoever in the diary that Mabel experiences boredom or frustration or a yearning for something other than what she has and is.

Mabel's personal commitment to the Christian faith is clear. She is involved in many aspects of her father's ministry both generally and at times of crisis. Mabel visits the sick and those about to die. She makes consistent efforts to help others to come to faith and is a staunch supporter of a life based on the principles of temperance. Mabel prays on her own and with friends, she reads the Bible and is regular in her attendance at church. Mabel is involved with the choir for which she plays the organ and she is supportive of the Church's missionary endeavour.

Mabel's diary for 1887

'Lovely day. Father gave me this book.' So Mabel Ridout begins her diary for January 1st 1887. Quite possibly the diary had been a recent Christmas present. Mabel's father had inscribed his gift 'With her father's love'. How little either Mabel or her father could have imagined that the gift would have survived more than 130 years, nor, indeed, that it might be accessible to read by anyone else.

With her father's love

The diary is entitled 'A Christian Remembrancer'[5]. It is a small book suitable for pocket or purse[6]. The first 30 or so pages of the diary are filled with words of devotional encouragement. There is also a brief almanac. Each week of the year is given a double page in which on one side is printed the days and dates together with a Bible text, while the other side is left blank. Mabel very often extended her writing onto this

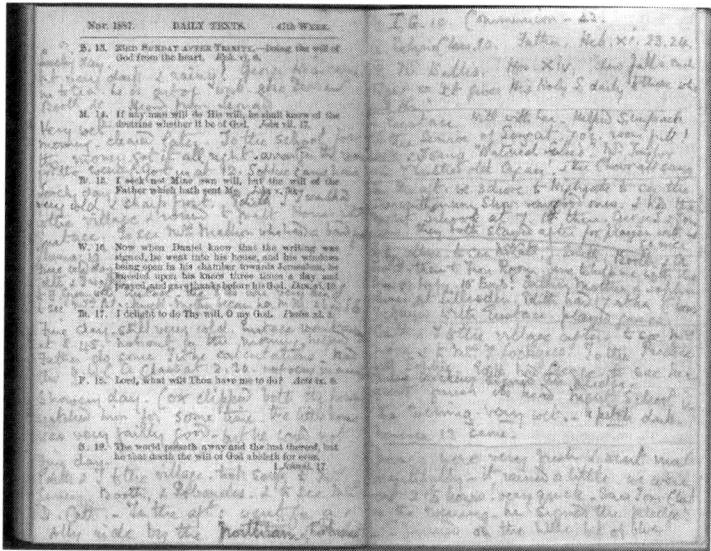

page. There is a Latin saying on the title page – 'Nulla Dies Sine Linea', which may be literally translated as

'Not a single day without a line'. Mabel very nearly achieved this goal[7]. Like many diarists of her time and, indeed later, Mabel chose to write in pencil[8]. There seem to be few, if any, occasions where she has made any amendments.

After 1887

After 1887 Mabel continued both to live in Sandhurst and keep a diary. As the youngest child, and a girl, in the Ridout family there would have been expectations on Mabel as regards taking care of her aging parents. She was already supporting her father in his ministry as she had been doing all her life. All but one of her siblings had gone from Sandhurst[9]. The ensuing years passed.

In 1907 Mabel's mother, Sophia, died followed by her father, George, in the following year. He was 88 years old and had been the Rector of Sandhurst for more than half a century. So came to an end the only sort of life that Mabel had ever known. She had been born in the Rectory and spent all her 42 years there as the Rector's daughter. It must have been a difficult and, perhaps, frightening time for Mabel. Left without parents and the only home that she had ever known, Mabel must have wondered what the future held for her. Made homeless as possession of the Rectory now passed to the next incumbent Mabel moved to the nearby village of Goudhurst[10].

In fact, a course of events which were something really rather remarkable were about to develop in Mabel's life. Within little more than 2 years Mabel was married and she chose a clergyman, The Reverend Sidney Smith, as her husband[11]. Mabel and Sidney were

married at All Souls, Langham Place in London on 23rd January 1911. Her relatively late arrival at matrimony was a significant event in itself, of course, but what was to happen next certainly added to matters. Just 2 days after their marriage the newlyweds boarded the SS Burutu bound for Forcados in Nigeria where they were to spend the next 14 years as missionaries with the Church Mission Society. It was one of the most dangerous and difficult mission postings anywhere in the world with many life threatening diseases being endemic to the region.

For Mabel all this was a far cry from the peace of the Kent countryside and the security and predictability of the life she had known in the Rectory and which she had only recently left. To make such a change at a relatively later stage in life, she was now 44, speaks volumes of Mabel's integrity, personal courage and faith. Mabel's diary shows that as a young woman she had been a committed supporter of missionary work

through her fundraising activities in Sandhurst and here she was now on the Niger Mission of West Equatorial Africa, a missionary herself.

With her father's love

The couple returned to England in 1925 and lived in retirement until Sidney's death in 1946. They had been married for 35 years. Mabel was to die in 1950 in Cambridge, aged 83.

Mabel was one of that generation whose lives seem to coincide with a period of great change in the world. She was born before the typewriter was invented yet lived to see the Atomic Age.

Mabel's diary for 1887 provides a window into just one year in a long and faithful life. It came 'With her father's love'.

Notes

1. The Wealden village of Sandhurst is located on the border between Kent and East Sussex some 18 miles south east of Tunbridge Wells. The main road from London to Rye runs through the village. It is a pretty and historic village with white wooden houses the architecture of which is characteristic of that part of Kent. Many local houses date from the 16th – 18th Century and some are even older. Sandhurst is surrounded by the beauty of the Kent countryside. The Church of St. Nicholas was originally established around the 13th - 14th Century. Although it stands nearly in the centre of the parish, on a hill, it is actually located at Sandhurst Cross about a mile from the village centre. The church is built of sandstone under a tiled roof and is a Grade II Listed Building. It enjoys the most glorious of views.

2. George Ridout had been educated at Emmanuel College, Cambridge. After ordination he served as curate at St George's, Bloomsbury, London and also as perpetual curate in the parish of Ash, near Sandwich, Kent. He became Rector of Sandhurst in 1857, a post which he then held for over half a century. George and Sophia were married on 22nd May 1848 at St George's, Bloomsbury, London.

3. George and Sophia had 9 children including Mabel. The others were: Mary Sophie, Emily Daniell, Arthur George, John Herbert (who died in

With her father's love

1881 aged only 26), Edith Caroline, Charles Edward, Evelyn Mary and Leonard. The servants variously comprised a Cook, Parlour Maid, House Maid and Kitchen Maid.

4. According to the 1881 Census, Mabel and her sister, Mary, lived at the Rectory but by that for 1891 it was Mabel and Evelyn.
5. The diary was published by Suttaby's of Amen Corner adjacent to St Paul's in London. At the time the area was the centre of the London publishing trade.
6. It is a handsome diary with gilt edging to the pages and a soft dark brown leather cover. Mabel's tiny writing within the diary extends to some 30, 000 words. For example, on a double page measuring 15 x 12 cm Mabel is able to record in excess of 450 words for the period 13th – 19th November. It is really quite an achievement.
7. The only dates with nothing recorded are for 7th & 8th January, 12th April and 30th & 31st December.
8. The pencil has long been the choice of many diarists. Nella Last, famously Housewife 49, who contributed her many diaries to the Mass Observation, wrote everything in pencil.
9. Mabel's sister, Evelyn.
10. About 9 miles from Sandhurst.
11. Sidney was born in Benenden, Kent in 1873. His family later moved to nearby Goudhurst. Unconventionally for the time Sidney was some 7 years younger than Mabel. He had a merited church ministry and was later to become an Archdeacon.

JANUARY

Saturday 1st

Lovely day. Cold. Father gave me this book. Heard from Dora. Out ferreting with Charlie & Leonard. They got 7 rabbits. To the village with Edith to see Mrs Simes & Mrs Judge. The bells rang in the evening.

Sunday 2nd

Lovely day. To play at the School in the morning. To church twice and to Sunday School in the afternoon. Began Mrs Brook's hymnbooks. To the Iron Room with Father & Emily. Edith had 15.

Monday 3rd

Wet day – thaw. Made a pair of cuffs and began a comforter. Went through the Xmas tree things and packed them into boxes ready to go down. Very cloudy & cold in the evening.

Tuesday 4th

Heavy fall of snow – 5 inches. Emily & Edith to the Iron Room at 10 30. Evelyn & I went down in the cart at 11. Had luncheon at the Taylors. Put several things on the tree. Mrs Minn helped. Wrote to Margaret & Sarah. Heard from Kitty & a card from Major Poole.

Wednesday 5th

Wet & thawing early – freezing hard later. Evelyn & I to Bryants' Cottage. Christmas Fire[1] at 6 30. 200

people. About 50 not there. All seemed very happy and to enjoy it thoroughly. Sunday School children, Mothers' Meeting, Sunday School teachers, Choir, Working Party, Band of Hope came. I gave mittens to P. Mallion & the comforter to A. Burt.

Thursday 6th The Epiphany[2]

Cold day. Emily, Edith & Evelyn went down and took the things off the tree. Mother for a drive to Field Green. Emily, Edith & I stayed together.

Friday 7th

Nothing recorded.

Saturday 8th

Nothing recorded.

Sunday 9th

Morning Father Fine day. To church in the morning. Stayed at home alone in the afternoon. Mrs Neve came to tea. Father, Emily & Edith to the Iron Room. Heard from Emma Emery.

Monday 10th

Fine day. Helped Sophie pack up. Mother, Charlie & Leonard to London to 19 Upper M. Street[3]. Leonard to see about Mains Electric Engineering. To Y.W.C.A.[4] meeting. Edith took Joshua chapter I. Very nice there. Arthur went up to London.

Tuesday 11th

Foggy day. Evelyn & I to see Mrs Shoesmith. Showed her my Xmas cards. And saw hers. Played backgammon with Evelyn. Mother to luncheon with the Pococks & to tea with the Fanshawes. She saw Mabel.

Wednesday 12th

Very wet day. Edith only had 3 at the Mothers' Meeting. Did not go out at all. Charlie came home in the evening. Heard from Mabel North-Row. Mabel F to luncheon at 19 Upper M Street.

Thursday 13th

Fine day. In the garden in morning. Laid down before tea. Practice in the house at 7 30. Charlie & Evelyn for a long ride. Had the Working Party. 4 came. Arthur returned to Newcastle.

Friday 14th

Fine day. Did not get up very early – I stayed in all day. Laid down a good deal.

Saturday 15th

Fine day. Very cold East wind. Not so well. Did not get up until late. The Boys came for the Band of Hope and they played with bricks & soldiers. Charlie & Edith to skate at Bay Pond. Heard from Maudie.

Sunday 16th

Fine day. Did not get up until 11. Edith stayed with me in the morning. Not at all well. Very cold. John Burt to the Sunday School twice!

Monday 17th

Lovely day. Very cold, indeed. Did not get up until 11. Charlie, Edith & Evelyn had some good skating at Bay

Pond. Mother came home in the evening. Emily to meet her.

Tuesday 18th

Fine day – very damp. Charlie went for a short ride. Edith & Evelyn began a reading at the Iron Room.

Wednesday 19th

Fine day. Better. Went out with Mother for a little. Evelyn & Charlie rode. To the Mothers' Meeting Tea. Mrs Annersley came down. Edith only had 6.

Thursday 20th

Lovely day. Charlie went back to Mortimer. Evelyn to the station with him. Went in the carriage as far as Field Green then laid down. Felt rather better. Practice in the house. Most of them learnt 'Now the day is over'[5].

Friday 21st

Fine day. Out for a little after dinner. Mother took Mrs Annersley for a ride. She brought a lovely work-case and was so kind.

Saturday 22nd

Fine day. Evelyn went for a ride with Cox. Mother & Emily to Field Green to meet Mrs Oakes! Had the Band of Hope for Girls. 11 came. Edith read to them. Did some more marking. Heard from Margaret. Evelyn's birthday.

Sunday 23rd

Father's birthday. Fine day. To church in morning. Began the 1st Class of Boys. Looked at the March verses. Mrs Neve here for tea.

Morning Father – Psalm ciii 13. Jesse Chantler & James Catt came into Choir.

Afternoon – Emily stayed with me.

Evening – Evelyn stayed with me – sang the Psalms.

L – 'Now the day is over'.

Monday 24th

Fine day. Emily & Evelyn to the school. Evelyn & I went out down to see the calves in the afternoon. Mother to Lillesden. Emily's birthday. Up to the Cottage at 6 30 for the Children's 'Bazaar'. Jane to see me.

Tuesday 25th

Lovely day. Went for a ride in the morning. Went up to see Mrs Shoesmith & Mrs Bryant. For a ride with Cox for an hour. Enjoyed it very much. The 5 Annersley children came down to tea – Willie, Arthur, Sophia, Philip & Eleanor. Played games with them until 7 15. Edith & Evelyn had about 30 or 40 people at the Iron Room. Mrs Walter Smith died. Wrote to Maggie & Miss Dingle.

Wednesday 26th

Lovely day. In the garden before 10 o/c. To the Mothers' Meeting & tea. 14 there. To see Mrs J Verrall. Out with Mother later. Evelyn for a drive with Mrs Annersley & the children.

Thursday 27th

Foggy early. Lovely later. To church in morning. Cut out 2 pinafores. Evelyn for a ride with Cox. Mother, Emily, Evelyn & I to Field Green. D'A's were out. Heard from Selina with a pretty apron. Working Party. 9 came, 4 fresh ones. Practice at church – all the men there.

Friday 28th

Fine day. In the garden in the morning. Sophia Annersley & the baby came to luncheon. Drove with Evelyn to the Lower End & to F. Green. D'A's were out. Heard from Mrs Legg. Wrote to Charlie & Emmie. My new dress came from Miss Panniers.

Saturday 29th

Damp, foggy day. Up to the church in the morning. Read German. Made some cough mixture. Mrs D'A & Mabel came in the afternoon & stayed to tea. Helped Mother with accounts. Band of Hope for Boys. Only 4. Mrs W. Smith buried.

Sunday 30th

Lovely day. To church. Mrs D'A & Mabel came to tea. Looked out texts I need. 'Fullness of blessing'.

Morning Father. Acts ix 1-4.

Afternoon Mr A Luke xviii 11. Had 8 boys at my class.

Evening Father Luke xii. Had the new Magnificat & chanted the Psalms[6].

Monday 31st

Dull day. Mother & Edith to Highgate. Did some Greek & out with Evelyn. Down to Old Place to see Jane & Mrs Shoesmith. Mother got Sophie's letter. Gave Judge a pair of mittens. Mrs Oakes, Mrs D'A, Mrs Weld & Mrs Simes came to arrange about the Jubilee. Mrs Clark died at Benenden.

FEBRUARY

Tuesday 1st

Wet day. Out in the garden for ½ an hour. Afterwards a good deal of marking. Mother read us John Halifax[7].

Wednesday 2nd

Lovely day. To the Cottage with Mother. Evelyn rode with Cox. Walked as far as Castle Gate with Emily & then up to old Osbourne with soup. Mothers' Meeting. 15. Helped at tea. Boys' Class – only 6. <u>Wet.</u>

Thursday 3rd

Showery day. To fetch Sophie & Nelly A. to luncheon. Mother took them for a drive. To the village with Emily – wet walk home. Wrote to Sophia. To see Mrs Gasson, Judge & Simes. Practice in the hall. Spoke to A. Burt.

Friday 4th

Fine day. Edith went to London. Mr & Mrs Annersley dined here & drove with Evelyn to Newenden. Wrote to Mabel N. Row. To see Fanny Catt with Mother – she looked so bright, but very ill.

Saturday 5th

Lovely Spring day. Evelyn drove with Mabel D'A. Mrs Clark buried at 3 30. Arranged the choir books. Sophia A. to tea. Finished 'Wives & Daughters'[8]. Band of

Hope. 10 girls. Then to see Mrs J. Smith, F. Catt & Mrs Verrall. Edith went to see Mabel F.

Sunday 6th

Fine day. Played hymns & read in the afternoon. Edith to P.C. twice!

Morning Communion 51. To play the hymns at Sunday School.

Afternoon To the Sunday School. 8 boys & then home.

Evening To the Iron Room with Father & Mother. I played. Lovely night.

Monday 7th

Fine day. Had a little cold. Gazy came to luncheon & Mrs M. came over to tea. The Annersleys also came to tea. Gazy took the Y.W.C.A. Very nice on the Law of God. Psalm cxix 'According to thy Word'.

Tuesday 8th

Fine day. Evelyn went to luncheon at Field Green. Walked across to see Mrs Mallion. Mrs Stedman was there. The drawing room chimney caught fire. Heard from Maude Matthews. Wrote to Mrs Springett. Also to Arthur. Mother & Evelyn to the Reading at the Iron Room.

Wednesday 9th

Fine day. Cold North East wind. To see Fanny Catt. Mrs A. Catt was there. Had a long talk with James Mallion. Worked the knitting machine. Wrote to Edith & Selina. Mothers' Meeting. 13 in the hall. Bible Class. Iron Room. Evelyn took it - 8.

Thursday 10th

Fine day. Bitter East wind. Minnie Tuck, Fitz & Dicky called. Put off the Practice. Mother & Emily to stay with the Maynards. Wrote to F. Corrie. Had the Working Party. 11 came! Mother & Evelyn returned.

Friday 11th

Fine. Very cold. Made 1 pair of socks for S. Arthur, May, Edith & Leonard came home. So nice to see them. Played games in the evening. To see Fanny Catt upstairs. Read 4 hymns to her. 'Lean hard', 'Just as I am', 'God will take', 'There is a blessed home'[9]. She said she was quite ready to go whenever the call came. I little thought it would be so soon.

Saturday 12th

Lovely day. Cold. We all went up to the church in the morning. Mother, Arthur, May & Evelyn to Field Green. They were out. The Oakes called. Leonard for a ride. Prepared my lesson on Acts I. Fanny Catt passed away at 12 15. Emily & Edith went there.

Sunday 13th

To the Sunday School. Mr Niel spoke to the whole school, Minnie Tuck for tea. Leonard & I walked up to Downgate with her. To the Iron Room with Father.

Monday 14th

Fine day. Out with Arthur & May. To see Mrs Cox & Field. In Ives Wood found some primroses. Arthur & Nicky to Lillesden & F. Green. To the village with Edith.

Took a message to Mrs Catt & then to Mrs Taylor. A. Field <u>out</u>. School. Mrs Vaughan & Mrs Judge.

Tuesday 15th

Fine day. Arthur & Leonard went away. Mr Niel gave a lecture on Palestine, very interesting. Showed some pictures. Walked back with May & Edith. Wrote to Johnnie Bryant & Maudie. Heard from F. Corrie. To see Mrs Shoesmith, old Osbourne, W. Burt, C. Burt, Catt & Jane & L. Moore.

Wednesday 16th

Lovely day. Evelyn for a ride. Father, Mother, Emily, May, Edith & I walked to Bodiam Castle[10]. We went inside. Drove with May to the village & Sponden. To the Mothers' Meeting Tea. 17. Edith's Bible Class 14.

Thursday 17th

Lovely day. Made a wreath of snowdrops. Took it to C. Gate. May & Edith walked there with me. Mother took May for a drive. Fanny Catt's funeral at 3 30. All the family there. The 1st Class Girls & Jane sang 'Safe in the arms of Jesus'[11] at the open grave. Very nice. The 4 bearers were John Mallion, Hegben, J. Chantler & J. Catt. Wrote to Sophie.

Friday 18th

Wet day. Evelyn & May left here at 11 15 to Boston. Missed them very much. Worked at the knitting machine. Made Mother's stockings. Heard from Maudie. Wrote to Mabel N. Row.

Saturday 19th

Fine day. For a ride with Cox at 11 20. Went by Fox Hole & Iden Green. Out 1 ¾ hours. Enjoyed it very much. Had some capital gallops. Up to the church later. Heard from dear Kitty. Boys Band of Hope – 5!

Sunday 20th

Fine day. To church & Sunday School.

Morning   Father 1st Girls. 9. 8 Boys.

Wrote to Evelyn.

Afternoon Genesis XII

Evening Mr Everett, very nice address on Psalm XL 'He brought me. He did it all'.

Monday 21st

Lovely day. The drawing-room turned out. Made Clara's stockings on the machine. For a drive with Mother in the afternoon.

Tuesday 22nd

Fine day. Practised for nearly an hour. Had luncheon early. Mother, Emily, Edith & I to Cranbrook. Lovely drive & saw Mrs Milton. In the evening Edith & I to the Reading at the Iron Room – about 20 there. I read Luke X & played. Edith read about the Good Samaritan.

Wednesday 23rd

Fine day. Drove Father to Alderden. Saw Dr & Mrs Slaughter & daughter. Made a 2nd pair of stockings for Clara. John Catt to see us. To the Mothers' Meeting

Tea – only 12. Service at church at 7. Father preached on Joel II. A. Burt & his wife there!

Thursday 24th

Fine day. For a ride to Arnold's & back by Fowlers Lane. Passed a traction engine![12] Mother & Emily to F. Green. Miss Elsam came here for one night. Working Party at 7. Walked up the shrubbery with Jane. John left home today. Practice 7 30 church. Very good one. Amos Catt came in after & I had a little talk with him. May he be lead to seek Jesus. Heard from Evelyn.

Friday 25th

Fine day. Mrs Elsam went away. Worked the knitting machine. For a drive with Father & Mother. To see Mrs Jempson & on to Hope House & the Lower End! Wrote to Mrs Rogers & sent some flowers.

Saturday 26th

Lovely day. Up to the church in the morning with Edith. Wrote the Choir papers. Made some more socks. Mr Perry came here. & Leonard surprised us as he had a bad cold. Played backgammon. Anne made some more marmalade.

Sunday 27th

Fine day. Mr Perry spoke to the children upon 2 Kings V. Stayed at home with Father & L in the evening.

Morning Psalm CXXII. I

Afternoon Genesis XIX. 17

Evening   Mr Perry spoke at the Iron Room.

Monday 28th

Lovely day. Mr Perry went away. Leonard & I went for a jolly ride with Mabel D'A. Out in the garden with Mother. The others to Bodiam. Had the 3 basses for Practice. John Matthews, G. Head & H. Osbourne.

MARCH

Tuesday 1st

Lovely day – quite warm. Mother & Emily to Hastings for the day. L. went with them & back to London[13]. Wrote to Kitty. To see Mrs Mallion. Edith & I to the reading at the Iron Room. I read Luke XVI & Edith read about it.

Wednesday 2nd

Rather foggy day. Out in the garden & up to the organ with Edith in the afternoon. Had a kind letter from Mrs Rogers. Mothers' Meeting. 15 to the Tea. Bible Class at Iron Room. 16.

Thursday 3rd

Very foggy. Made 3 stockings for Anne. To the village in the afternoon to see Mrs Piper, P. Milton James, J. Nash, A. Burt, Vaughan, Wickens & Mrs Bailey. Had the Practice in the house. Not many there.

Friday 4th

Foggy. Partly cleared later. Covered down marmalade. Wrote to Dora. Drove down to the Lower End & walked back to see Mrs Hodge, Mrs Robards, Mrs Coleman, Mr Ballard, Crisford, Mrs Christmas & to Mrs Simes. Had the boys for practice.

Saturday 5th

Fine day. Went for a jolly ride with Cox by Bodiam Junction & the Brick Kilns. Read & worked in the evening. Heard from M. North Row. Only 3 boys at Band of Hope. Dora's birthday.

Sunday 6th

Fine day. To church 3 times. Psalms chanted in the morning & hymns. 82 in the Book.

Morning Communion 39

Afternoon Father. Had the 1st Boys.

Evening Mr Fenn. Matthew XXVII. 22. What shall I do then with Jesus? Question for each – most solemn.

Monday 7th

Fine day. Mother & Father went off at 7 30. To the church in morning & to call at Downgate with Emily. Y.W.C.A. 13 at it. Very nice about Rahab[14]. Had the 4 tenors for practice. Amos Catt came in after tea for a 'draught'. Talked about bees. Gave him 'Crossing the bridge'.

Tuesday 8th

Lovely day. Went in the carriage to the village. To see Mrs Judge, Mrs Taylor, Mrs Seny & Job Catt. Wrote to Evelyn & Miss Dingle. Sent the latter some violets. Edith & I to our Reading – more there. Read Psalm XXIII & John X.

Wednesday 9th

Fine day. Worked the knitting machine. Edith took the Mothers' Meeting. 12 there. Took Anne for a drive. Edith had 16. Heard from Dora. Evelyn to Wilford from Boston.

Thursday 10th

Fine day. Emily & Edith for a drive to Hawkhurst. Mabel D'A to tea. Walked back with her later. Heard from Mother. Then the Working Party. 7 there. Practice in the house – very good one. All there except Amos & Willie Catt.

Friday 11th

Lovely day. To the church in the morning – picked some violets. Heard from Evelyn. Played backgammon with Edith. Cox drove us to the Lower End. I to see Miss Collins (Stone House), Mrs Christmas, Mrs Larkin, Mrs Moore, Mrs James, Mrs Lade & D. Catt.

Saturday 12th

Fine day. Snowy & very cold. The carriage went for the 12 19 train & Father did not come down till the Xpress. Only 4 girls at the Band of Hope. Down to Old Place with Emily. Paid Jane a long visit. Talked of Romans XIV. Father came home with a very bad cold. Evelyn joined Mother in London.

Sunday 13th

Fine day & cold. To Sunday School & church twice. Chanted the Psalms & had the new Te Deum[15]. Had the Almanacs[16] with the girls.

Morning 1st Girls Genesis XXXVII. 3-4

Afternoon 1st Girls Luke XI. 14

Evening Capt. Brenton Job XXI

Monday 14th

Fine cold day – bright early. Emily & Edith to Mrs Rollings. Saw Jane in the evening for a few minutes. She gave me Daniel XII. 3 & Psalm 5. 12. To see Mrs Judge. School. Mrs A. Field & Mrs Taylor.

Tuesday 15th

Very snowy day. Up to see Mrs Shoesmith. Father took the wedding of Miss Bruce & Glen Nash. It cleared a little in the afternoon. Eva Locock confirmed. To see Mrs Roberson with Emily. Edith & I to our Reading. Only 12 there. Cold evening. Read Daniel IX 'Prayer'. Corrected the Home Study papers.

Wednesday 16th

Snowy early. Fine later. To see Mrs Field, Mrs Verrall & Mrs Shoesmith. The latter gave me Proverbs XIV. 26. Jane to say goodbye. She brought me some violets and primroses. Edith had the Mothers' Meeting in the hall. Only 8. She had 9 at her Bible Class. Albert Burt came in after. Gave him some cough mixture. He is not yet fully satisfied - but anxious.

Thursday 17th

Fine. Very cold. Rather snowy. Packed up. Picked some violets. Mr & Mrs Annersley came down. Left home at 3 15. Emily with me. Came up by the 4 22 train. Got to Charing X at 6 24 & to 19, Upper M. Street before 7. Found Evelyn & Leonard in. Mother went home by the express. Passed her near Tunbridge Wells. Evelyn went to tea with the Lococks.

Friday 18th

Fine & cold. Went out at 9 with Evelyn. Saw over an organ factory in Marylebone Road[17]. Then Evelyn practised till 11. To luncheon with Flossie at 1. Lovely house – saw Mrs Sheepshanks & the 3 children. Mr S played the organ to me. Then to Mrs Sawle's, Mrs Harvey's & Mrs Woollands'. Saw Emily Wild for a moment. Saw several grand carriages returning from the Drawing Room. Home by bus. Wrote to Mother. Got a new pair of stays. 16/6[18].

Saturday 19th

Fine & rain. Heard from Evelyn. Out at 11 to Mrs Stanford's, Mrs Pannier's, Mrs Novello's. Lunch at 2 when Leonard came in. We all went out at 3 30. First to Upper Grosvenor Street. Found Aunt May had left. To Dover Street. Left the book. Then when we got to Hyde Park Corner found a crowd & the Queen was coming! Got good places & saw the Lifeguards followed by a carriage with 4 horses in which was the Queen! Princess Beatrice & Prince Henry[19]. Saw them well. Then on to Eaton Square. Saw Uncle John, Sybil

& Maud – had tea there. Walked home across the Park & to see the Hesses. Went home.

Sunday 20th

Lovely day. In the afternoon walked to Gloucester Square. All out. Met Lucy & went in for ½ an hour. Dora & all the others got out. M to P Chapel. Mr Sherbrooke Psalm CIII. 11-13. Edith to St. Anne's, Soho. Beautiful singing. Anthem 'Fear not, O land' Canon Wade preached poor sermon. Mr Horsley preached 2nd (at home) & Col. Driver spoke in the evening. Collection £7^{20}. Wrote to Edith.

Monday 21st

Fine day. To St Mary's with Evelyn for her organ lesson at 9 10. Then out walked down to Mrs Bennett's, made an appointment & then to Panzetta's. Measured for boots. After luncheon, to see Miss Dingle & Miss Hall. Mrs Taylor had a little boy. Wrote to Edith. Then walked across the Park to Halkin Street West. Met May on the doorstep. Saw Mrs Fanshawe & Kit. Several people calling. Severely cold. Hurried back expecting that she did not come! Note from Dora. Wrote to Edith. Missionary Meeting at home.

Tuesday 22nd

Showery. Much warmer. I heard from Emily. Wrote to Mother. Went out at 11 30. Walked to Dobb's. Got riding gloves & veil. Then to Mrs Pulls where we stayed to luncheon! Walked across the Gardens to see G. Wilde. Then to Mrs Sawles. She was out! To Hawleys & Woodhams then to call on the Parkers where we had tea & rested. Rained heavily all the way back.

Wednesday 23rd

Fine day. To Evelyn's organ lesson at 9 10. Heard from Kitty & Edith. To P. C. at 12. Mr Rice preached on Ephesians 3. Copied some sermon notes & then out again at 3 to Morley Halls. Y.W.C.A. Spoke to Mrs Athill. Mr George Clarke gave a splendid address on Zechariah XIII.6 'Wandering Jesus' Found Maude & Edie Matthews in alone. Had tea with them. Then I began a letter to Emily. To St Anne's, Soho at 8 to hear Bach's Passion Music (St John). Very lovely.

Thursday 24th

Showery day. Wrote to Emily & Charlie. Out at 10 15 to see the Hesses then on to Hamptons where we met May & chose 2 dresses for Emily & me. 30/- tack[21]. Then to the Haywards & S.P.C.K.[22] & on to the Army & Navy[23] where we had lunch. Then to Mrs Sawles. Tried on both our dresses. Came up in a bus from Hyde Park Corner & got in at 5 20! Very tired & footsore. Began to write some geography questions & played duets with Evelyn.

Friday 25th

Fine day. Evelyn to her organ lesson at 9 till 9 45. Then she met Jane Catt at Charing X who bought us lovely flowers, eggs, cake & coffee. I to Mr Bennett's. He stopped 2 teeth. Then to luncheon with the Lococks. Saw them all. I heard Mr Carruthers give a most interesting address on the Tabernacle[24] & show a model. Blanche to tea with us at 4 o/c. Rained heavily later.

Saturday 26th

Lovely day. I to Mr Bennett's at 9 30. Wrote to Mother. Out at 10 15. To Treefits. Had our hair cut. To Haywards for luncheon & to the Junior Army & Navy. Met Annette at Westminster at 2 after queuing into the Abbey for 20 minutes. Annette took us all over her hospital. Everything so nice & pretty & all the patients looked so happy. Walked back around Hyde Park. Leonard went to see the Boat Race. Cambridge won! Then we went to tea with the H. Hills. Wrote to M. Carter.

Sunday 27th

Lovely early. Snowy later. E. to St Anne's in the morning & to St Peter's, Eaton Square in the evening. Wrote to Edith & to Kitty. Mr Tun at home. Morning Parish Church. Mr Sherbrooke Luke II. 36-38. Afternoon. Walked first to St Giles but found Mr Stuart's service was for Men Only[25]. Then to All Saints, Margaret Street for a little rest & then to the Y.W.C.A. Mr Dashwood gave a splendid address on Romans IV 2. Evening. Mr Stuart took whole service & preached 2 Peter I. 5.

Monday 28th

Lovely day. Evelyn to the organ session at 9. I practised. Heard from M. Carter. Wrote to Kitty & Mother. Out at 10 30. Walked along Lisson Grove & Abbey Road to see Charlotte Mallin first then to see the Underhills & to the Henderson's Nursery. To luncheon with the Hesses at 1 30. Then I went to call on Mrs Athill. She came in about ½ an hour. I stayed some time with her. So nice & kind. Then to call on Miss Wood with Evelyn & P. Merchison. <u>Out.</u> Emily Wilde to tea with us.

Tuesday 29th

Fine day. Wrote to Mother. Heard from her. To Novello's & Miss Panniers in the morning. Then in for 1 hour. Walked across the Park to Halkin Street. Found May alone at first. Had luncheon & then so cut up to see all the presents. Great many. Some lovely ones. Then to order our hats & the Junior Army & Navy. Got in soon after 6. Played duets in the evening.

Wednesday 30th

Fine day. To the organ session with Evelyn. Went to see the Hesses. They were just starting for home. Met Dora at 11 30. Saw Miss White & May Robinson. To Parish Church at 12. Mr Hindley preaching on Isaiah LVIII. 21. Nice sermon. Mary Witherby to see us. To Mr Clarke's meeting at 3 30. Very nice address on Hebrews XIII.8. Jesus as Saviour, Deliverer, Shepherd. Walked back with Miss Athill. In the evening walked down to Holborn. Saw Flossie, Mrs Sybil, Maude & Blanche. Wrote to Jane & Emma Emery.

Thursday 31st

Fine early. Wet later. Out in the morning for a little while. Walked down Regent Street in the afternoon. Walked to Edgware Road. Evelyn went down to Walthamstow at 5 o'c. Mildred C. met me. Saw Mr & Mrs Carter, Mabel, Rose & Gertrude. Dinner at 6 30 then out to hear Mr Hastings lecture. Most interesting.

APRIL

Friday 1st

Showery. Left 'The Limes' at 11. Evelyn joined me at Liverpool Street. Walked to Paternoster Row. Then to St Paul's. Heard Canon Body. Had luncheon & on to Exeter Hall. Got good seats for the Children's Scripture Union Meeting[26]. Mr Stuart, Chairman, gave a nice address on the 'finest chamber'. Wane Davis (Honolulu) & Arrowsmith spoke. Enjoyed it very much. Came back in a bus. Leonard got back very late & brought the book cases.

Saturday 2nd

Lovely day. Went into Baker Street and then I went to see Dora. They kept me to luncheon and I saw them all. At 2 & we went at once to Steinway Hall to hear Clifford Harrison recite. Splendid. Then we walked to Halkin Street. The presents all laid out. A splendid quantity & many fresh ones. Saw Mrs Fanshawe & Evelyn. Also the Smith Bosanquets & Mrs Pering. Stayed on talking to May & Evelyn till 7 30. Got home rather late.

Sunday 3rd Palm Sunday[27]

Lovely. Warm day. Evelyn to lunch in Halkin Street. We met Mrs Fanshawe & Kit & went to the zoo with them. Saw all the animals & enjoyed it. Mrs Fanshawe gave us 2 lovely feathers. They came to tea with us. Mrs Knight at home. M to Parish Church with Evelyn. Mr

Sherbrooke preached. We stayed to the Communion. Evelyn to Parish Church again. Mr S continued morning's sermon. Leonard went to Brompton Oratory[28] in the morning.

Monday 4th

Lovely day again. Packed up all the morning. The carpenter came to finish the bookcases. Did up the bath. Then to see the Hesses & on to the Parish Church for service. Mr Rice preached!! Stayed to speak to Mr Sherbrooke. He was *so* kind & nice. Evelyn & I walked down to Charing Cross. Came home by 3 55. & got in at 6 30. Very glad to get here.

Tuesday 5th

Wet day & much colder. Unpacked & tidied own room. In the afternoon went up to the church to see Mrs Shoesmith & Mrs Bryant. They helped Emily sow some seeds. It rained heavily later. Edith went alone.

Wednesday 6th

Very wet all day. No Mothers' Meeting. Did not get out at all. Edith went down to her class – only had 1! Charlie came home in the evening. Copied out several copies of a hymn for Edith.

Maundy Thursday 7th

Fine day & cold East wind. Edith & I went out at 11 to see Mrs Robbards & Mrs Mallion. Home by the fields – Charlie & Leonard went for a ride. No one came to the Working Party. Out in the garden with Mother. To the Practice at the church in the evening. Arthur came up to London. One lamb born.

Good Friday 8th

Fine day. To the church. In the afternoon. In the afternoon for a walk to the Kent Ditch[29] & home by the Dark Wood. Got some white violets & pansies.

Morning Father

Evening Father.

Saturday 9th

Fine day. Still very cold. Did some drawing & practised. Up to the church. Emily & Edith did some decorating. They got a good many flowers. Helped Evelyn get some flowers for the Dining Room. Arthur came home in the evening. Mother to meet him in the brougham. Had a note from Sarah telling me of her brother's death.

Easter Day 10th[30]

Lovely day. To church & to Sunday School twice. Took the '1st Class Girls' both times.

Morning Communion 54

Afternoon Father preached

Evening Father preached

Mr Annersley helped Father each time. Arthur Bryant's baby christened.

Easter Monday 11th

Fine day. Packed up my basket. We all left home at 11 0'c. Father, Mother, Emily & I in the fly & the rest in the waggonette. Very hot morning. Got to Charing Cross at 2. Saw Mrs G. Mallion to London. All the demonstration people to the Park[31]. Evelyn & I went straight up to the Hesses & Leonard came to sleep there. Father & Mr Arthur to Eaton Square. Emily & Edith to Mrs Julls & Charlie to an hotel. Evelyn dined in Halkin Street. Emily & Edith dined with us.

Tuesday 12th

!

Wednesday 13th

Fine day. Left Montagu Place at 11 30. Drove to Eaton Square. Found Mother very poorly. Out with Father for a walk to Halkin Street. Mother saw Mrs Fanshawe & Kit. Evelyn & I left London at 3 55. Father to see us off. Cox met us. Found Charlie all alone. He dined with Mr Neve. Anne & Clara came home early. Charlie rode.

Thursday 14th

Fine day. Up to the organ for 2 hours & to see Mrs Shoesmith. To the village in the afternoon. To see Mrs Taylor, Mrs Fellows & Mrs Field. Father & Mother came home in the evening. Evelyn & I to the Practice at the church. A good many there.

Friday 15th

Fine day. To the church in the morning. Father had a Vestry Meeting[32]. No more Godden. Lionel & Mabel came to lunch. To see Mrs Shoesmith after tea and to Old Place. Saw Mrs Catt. Mêt Jane near the church & talked to her for 30 minutes. Leonard came home in the evening.

Saturday 16th

Fine day. Mother heard from Arthur from Totnes. Leonard settled to go to Truro as master in a school. Heard from Maude Matthews. Up to the church in afternoon. Practised a good deal & prepared a lesson on the Tabernacle.

Sunday 17th

Fine day. To church & school & to the Iron Room. Played in the afternoon.

Morning Father

Afternoon Father Luke XXIV

Evening Father XXIV

Monday 18th

Fine day. To Old Place with Leonard to practise the organ. Evelyn to take the school money. Walked to Rock & Castle with them in the afternoon. They stayed to tea & Father drove her back to the 'Queens'. Charlie & Leonard dined at Field Green. I had the boys to practise at the Mission Room.

Tuesday 19th

Lovely day. South West Wind. Quite hot. To see Mrs Robbards, Mrs J. Catt, Mrs Judge & Mrs Mann. Sowed a good many seeds. Lionel & Mabel came over. Wrote to Dora. Lionel stayed to supper. We played 'Telegram' & other board games. Emily & Edith came home. Sent flowers to Annette. Primrose Day[33].

Wednesday 20th

Fine day. Put in some Sun Flower seeds. I picked flowers. Sent about 40 bunches to Miss Atthill. Wrote to her. Edith had the last class. She had 16 at her class. To Field Green. Walked there with Leonard. Mrs Neve & Mrs P. Cotterill. Practised rifle shooting. Drove Mother home. Mother heard from Arthur & May.

Thursday 21st

Lovely day. Sent flowers to Sybil & Mrs Underhill. Had the Working Party. 7 there. Kept Jane a little after. Lionel & Mabel came for tennis & tea. Father, Emily & Charlie dined at the Oakes'. To the Practice with Evelyn & Edith. Very good one. Charlie & Evelyn for a ride.

Friday 22nd

Dull day - it rained a little. Not out before luncheon. Tidied some drawers & marked a pair of sheets. Mrs Field to stay here. Wrote to Lovedy & Miss Douglas. The tanks were cleaned out. Mother to see Mrs Taylor.

Saturday 23rd

Lovely day. Charlie & I went for a ride in the morning. After luncheon, Emily & I to Old Place & Jane came out with us & we got a quantity of primroses. Did them up when we got home. Made 115 bunches. Old Moore died.

Sunday 24th

To church twice & to the Iron Room in the evening. Walked home with Jane. To the Sunday School twice.

Morning Mr Bushnell

Afternoon Father II Boys

Evening Mr Weatherly Joshua IV.

Monday 25th

Lovely morning but came on to rain later. In the shrubbery in the morning & got a quantity of primroses. Sent over 100 bunches to Miss Rogers by Father who went to Sevenoaks. Arthur & May returned to Halkin Street. In the afternoon Mrs Cox, Nellie & Bobbie came out to get primroses with us in the wood near the Sheep Pond. Jane came up to help us. Got very wet. The Simes, J, Schuler & C brought a good many flowers. Sent about 400 bunches to Mrs Sherbrooke.

Tuesday 26th

Fine day. Very cold. Leonard packed up & went off at 2. He dines in Halkin Street & goes by the night train to Truro. About the garden with Charlie. Father came back from Sevenoaks. Very wet evening. Evelyn & I to the Practice. Only 4 there. Began the 'Welcome' on calico[34].

Wednesday 27th

Fine day. Edith & I hard at work all day on the decorations at the gate. Put up 'Welcome' & evergreens around. Got a good many flowers for the house. A man from Goudhurst thatched the summer house & it looked so nice. Arthur & May arrived home at 6 30. The bells rang merrily. Edith to her class. 9 there.

Thursday 28th

Lovely morning. Charlie went back to Mortimer. About the garden with Arthur & May. To the Cottage summer house. Had the p. carriage at 3. Edith, Arthur & I walked to Sponden. Evelyn, Emily & May followed in the carriage. Went to Iden Green & round by Fox Hole. We all drove by turns. Got ferns[35] & flowers. It rained heavily all the way home. Jane came up in the evening & brought me lovely anemones.

Friday 29th

Fine day. Very cold. Arthur & May for a ride to Junction & Cripps Corner. Arranged some flowers & trimmed my hat. The summer house was finished. Cost £2. 0. 0[36]. Several people came at 3 30 to meet Arthur & May. Mrs D'A & Mabel, Mr & Mrs Oakes, Mr & Mrs French, A. Blanche, Mrs Loyd & Mary, Mrs Selmes & 2 misses, Mr Greenhill, Mr Maynard & Gazy, Mrs Springett & Edith. The D'A's stayed late. Evelyn & I to the Practice.

Saturday 30th

Lovely day. Still very cold. Arthur & May for a ride with Mabel D'A to Giles. To the church in the morning. Had the carriage at 2 30. Arthur, Edith & I walked to Risden. The others followed & brought Mrs D'A. We went down the lane behind Fowlers & got a splendid quantity of single Lent Lily roots[37]. Arthur, May, Evelyn & I to tea at F Green. Round the garden later. They gave us some lovely roses. Put some lace on my clean embroidery dress.

MAY

Sunday 1st

Fine. Bitterly cold wind. To church & Sunday School twice. Mr Neve to tea. In the shrubbery after. Got some flowers for them to take.

Morning Communion 41

Afternoon Father Job 42

Arthur read the lessons both times.

Evening Mr Knight gave a most solemn address on Luke XXIII. 40-43 'Dying thief'. Salvation is 1. Free 2. Immediate 3. Complete.

Walked home with Edith & Jane.

Monday 2nd

Showery day. Arthur & May left us at 8 30. Father & Mother packed up the table, sofa & beds to go to Newcastle. To the village in the afternoon. Evelyn walked to Castle Gate with me to see Mrs Judge, Mrs Taylor & Mrs Gasson. The Y.W.C.A. meeting was at 6 o'c. 18 attended. Edith took Joshua IV. Very nice. Had a little talk with Jane afterwards.

Tuesday 3rd

Lovely day. In the garden in the morning. Did a good deal of gardening and sowed some seeds. Mother, Edith & Evelyn drove to Hawkhurst. Went to see David Catt & Mrs Joe Catt. He has rheumatism, so pleased to see me. Did some weeding after tea. Arthur & May to Newcastle.

Wednesday 4th

Fine day. Cooler. Went for a jolly ride at 11 with Cox. Went to Iden Green & on by a lovely lane to just below Rolvenden. Splendid canter – enjoyed it immensely. Up to the Cottage Garden with Mother & Bryant. Tidied it & put in a few seeds. Edith had her last Bible Class & had 16!

Thursday 5th

Lovely day. Packed up our own things. Then out in the garden – planted the Lent Lilies. Had the Working Party in the Mission Room. 7 there. Jane came in later. Mother gave her a book-slide. She came up in the evening to see me – gave her Ezra IX. Sent a box of flowers to Mrs Atthill. Had a note from her.

Friday 6th

Very wet. Left home at 7 30 with Mother & Evelyn in the wagonette. Got to station in 45 minutes. Changed at Tunbridge Wells. Had an hour to wait & on to Brighton. Stayed there 1 ½ hours & came on to Ryde by 1 15 train. Had 1 hour to wait at Portsmouth ½ an hour more at Ryde Pier. Got to Lynwood at 6 30. Found Uncle A. & Aunt Gussie very well. Dinner at 7. To bed late.

Saturday 7th

Lovely day. Quite warm. Down to Union Street with Mother & Emily. Looked at the shops. Wrote to Leonard. In the afternoon Emily & I went for a walk in the Park & down to the Parade. Sat out a little while. Evelyn went for a jolly ride by the Junction & Cripps Corner.

Sunday 8th

Lovely day. Aunt Gussie went to the school twice. We went to St James. Heard Mr Redknapp. Father took two services at home & Mr Edwards in the evening.

Morning Mr Redknapp I Chronicles XI. 17

Did not go to church again. For a walk with Emily. Edith began her Sunday evening Bible Class – 21.

Monday 9th

Lovely day. Emily & I went on an Excursion Coach. We left the Pier Hotel at 11 & passed Binstead, Wootton, Quarr Abbey, Fishbourne, Whippingham, Osborne, Cowes to Newport, saw Whippingham Church. The on to Carisbrooke where we spent 2 hours to see the castle – drove back over Ashdown, Blackwater & Averton. Grand views in every direction.

Tuesday 10th

Lovely day. Had a carriage at 12 & Uncle, Mother, Emily & I drove to Sea View. Lovely drive. Walked along the sea wall. Got in at 2. Found a letter from Mildred written from Sea View! Wrote to Evelyn. Emily & I walked down to Union Street & got some dates for Mother. For a walk with Aunt Gussie.

Wednesday 11th

Lovely day. Wrote to May. Heard from Evelyn. Mother packed. Aunt Gussie & we 3 started by 11 o'c boat to

Portsmouth. Saw Mother off for home at 12. Had a boat. Went over the Victory & Duke of Wellington[38]. Both fine ships. 700 men on board the latter. Then by train to Southsea. Did some shopping & came back by the 6 o'c boat. It rained heavily for a time.

Thursday 12th

Fine day. Thundery. Wrote to Sophie. Heard from Dora. In the afternoon Emily & I walked to Sea View by the sea wall. Found Mildred had left yesterday. Came back by the lane. Lovely walk. Marked some of Uncle A's socks. Played backgammon with Aunt Gussie in the evening. Mr & Mrs Blenkin & Eunice to stay at home.

Friday 13th

Fine day. Much colder. Wrote to Mildred Carter. Got up early & wrote to Mother. Down to Union Street & bought several little things & did some commissions for Uncle A. Aunt Gussie went out with us after tea & we went to Union Street & High Street. Went round Dinnocks Nursery. Garden very pretty.

Saturday 14th

Fine day. Heard from Mrs Atthill. Wrote to Jane. Arranged some cowslips & primroses for Aunt Gussie. Then to Union Street for Uncle Arthur. In the afternoon out with Aunt Gussie & Emily. Walked to Spring Vale to see the Willowbank Garden. Lovely trees. Then to see some people at Puckpool. Came back along the sea wall then through St Clare & by the lanes again. Sea deep blue & had lovely peeps of it. Aunt Gussie gave us large bunches of cowslips to send away. Saw the Channel Squadron[39] arrive at Portsmouth – Minotaur (5 masts), Monarch & Sultan in the 7th Class[40].

Sunday 15th

Lovely day. To St James in the morning. To the Sunday School with Aunt Gussie. Had 6 girls in the 7th Class. Wrote to Edith. Sang hymns & looked out texts. Tied up the cowslips into 34 bunches.

Morning Mr Redknapp John XV.26 Mr Blenkin at home Daniel IX. 9-10

Mr Blenkin spoke in the Iron Room. Edith's class – 14.

Mrs A. Catt had a little son.

Monday 16th

Fine day. Not out in the morning. Worked at my slipper & marked some more clothes. In the afternoon Aunt Gussie & Emily & I went with Holly & Mary Pison, Mabel Stone & Miss Gilpin to Haven Street to get cowslips. Found 7 fields of them – splendid. Picked as many as we could. Had new milk & bread & butter at a farm ' 'Ome is 'ome & 'ome is everything'. Heard from Mother & Jane.

Tuesday 17th

Fine day. Went down to Ryde with Aunt Gussy & Emily. Heard from Mother & Mrs Harper. Did some shopping. To Halstead. In the afternoon we walked down again and went on toward Binstead. Wrote to Arthur & Mother. Emily Daniels & Mrs Holmes went home.

Wednesday 18th

Wet morning. Not out at all. Lined Uncle A's chimney piece border & Emily pasted in some scraps. The Blenkins left home. School inspected[41]. Wrote to Charlie & Miss Dingle. Down to Ryde in afternoon & bought several things at the Bazaar.

Thursday 19th Ascension Day[42]

Fine early. To church at 11. Mr Ewbank preached. Put up Uncle A's chimney piece. He showed us his nuggets of gold. Started to Ventnor & Bonchurch at 1 18. It poured with rain & we only went to see 2 churchyards & then returned. Packed up. To bed late.

Friday 20th

Very windy day. Left Lynwood at 9 30. Very sorry to come away. Aunt Gussie crossed with us. Had a good tossing which I enjoyed very much. Left Portsmouth at 12. Came by Brighton & St Leonards. Got home at 4 30. Very heavy hailstorm. Found Emily Daniel here. Very glad to get home. Unpacked. Mrs Shoesmith very ill.

Saturday 21st

Lovely day. Up to see Mrs Shoesmith before breakfast. Very ill. She knew me & spoke to me. I meant to ride but could not. The Co-op things came. Helped unpack them. Wrote to Leonard. Heard from Eva & Aunt Gussie. Worked at my slipper. Walked to Mrs Crouch's with Edith.

With her father's love

Sunday 22nd

Lovely day. Father, Mother & Emily went to see Mrs Shoesmith at 7 30 & she received the Communion.

Morning Mrs Shoesmith prayed for. Father Luke XXIV I Girls.

Afternoon Father John VII. 37. Had II boys.

Evening Father. Edith had 15.

Monday 23rd

Lovely day. In the garden in the morning. Finished our slippers. Wrote a note to Uncle A & sent them. Emily wrote to Aunt Gussie. Drove with Mother, Evelyn & Emily to Hawkhurst. Called at Lillesden - out. Mother & Evelyn to Field Green. Went in to see Mr Blackwell's Nursery.

Tuesday 24th

Fine day. To the village with Father in the morning. To old Leny. Very ill. We received the Communion. Solemn service. His cough was very bad. Evelyn took Emily & M. Goodsell for a drive. Went to see David Catt. Read to him & stayed some time. Heard from May – the first letter from her. Old George James buried.

Wednesday 25th

Fine day. Evelyn went for a ride with Cox. Down to Old Place to see Cox. Pulled up parsley. The fair at the village so stayed away. Did some gardening in the afternoon & worked at Aunt Gussie's side-board cloth. Jane came up to Edith's reading. Saw her after & had a nice talk with her in the shrubbery. Fetched 2 plants away from the Cottage. Wrote to Kitty.

Thursday 26th

Fine day. Up to the Cottage with Mother. Put up curtains. Heard from Kitty. Made a wreath of narcissus & forget-me-not. We all went to Mrs Shoesmith's funeral at 2 30. Good many people. Sang 'I heard the voice'[43]. There were several wreaths. Edith, Evelyn & I to tea at Field Green. Heard from Uncle Arthur. To see David Catt, read to him. To the Practice.

Friday 27th

Showery day. Not out in the morning. Wrote to Kitty. To the village with Emily in the afternoon. To the school. Mrs Amos Catt. She was pretty well. Saw the old man. Very ill indeed. Said some verses & 'I heard the voice' to him, which he understood. Then to Mrs Taylor's. Mrs Marshall died at 11 o'c. Bedridden 8 ½ years.

Saturday 28th

Fine day. Heard from Leonard & Kitty. Did a good deal of gardening. Planted the dahlias & several gladiolus. Mother. Emily & Emily D. went for a drive to Hawkhurst. Poor old Leny died at 12 o'c. To the church after tea. Cut the grass on our own darling's grave[44] & did a tin of white lilac. Finished the sideboard cloth for Aunt Gussie. Very wet afternoon.

Whit Sunday 29th[45]

Fine day. Not so warm. To church & Sunday School twice. Mrs Marshall was buried at 4 30. Copied some hymns. Edith had 18. Amos Catt there!

Morning Communion 51. Mr J. Newman was there. I Class Girls.

Afternoon Father John XIV.26 Had 9 of II Class Boys.

Evening Edith & Evelyn went to the service with Father. Mrs P. Mallion at church again.

Whit Monday 30th[46]

Fine day. Very close & thundery. To the organ at 11 for an hour. Turned out 3 cupboards. Mother, Emily D'A & Evelyn to tea at Field Green. Edith & I walked to see Mrs Mallion. The bees swarmed. I took them successfully. Pulled up a quantity of bindweed. After supper to the summer house.

Whit Tuesday 31st

Lovely day. To the station with Emily D. at 12 19. Horses <u>very</u> fresh & nearly ran away! Met Kitty & got in at 1 o'c. In the afternoon to see Mrs Cox & up to the organ for 1 hour. Evelyn fetched M. Goodsell back from Highgate. Helped Kitty unpack. Mrs Crouch died.

JUNE

Wednesday 1st

Lovely day. About the garden in the morning. Then to see the Cottage & down to Old Place with Kitty. Saw Jane for a few moments. The others drove to Mountfield. Stayed with Mother. To see Mrs Job Catt & Mrs Verrall. Then did some planting out. Looked through Mrs Shoesmith's clothes. Meant to have the Band of Hope but only Bobby came! Turk & Jock nearly fought[47]!

Thursday 2nd

Fine morning. Very wet later. Made a wreath of white lilac & forget-me-not for poor old Leny who was buried at 3 o'c. Too it up to Mrs Bryant. Had the Working Party at 2 30. Only 3 besides Clara & Mary. Mr & Mrs Horsley & 2 children arrived at the Cottage. He came down in the evening very merry! To the Practice with Evelyn. Very wet so only a few there.

Friday 3rd

Thoroughly wet day. Worked & read in the morning but could not go out. To the organ in the afternoon for 1 hour. Mr Horsley brought Etta (8) & Anna (6) down to tea. Dear little children. Had a nice letter from Aunt Gussie & my knife came back from Halstead.

With her father's love

Saturday 4th

Lovely day. To the organ at 10 30. Then down to Old Place. Took Etta & Anna with Kitty round the farm & garden. Saw Mrs Horsley for a few minutes. He went away for Sunday. For a drive in the afternoon to Highgate & to call on the Hardcastles & the Maynards. Mrs Crouch was buried. The bees swarmed. Searched for the Queen & found her! All the bees went back to the brown hive.

Sunday 5th Trinity Sunday[48]

Lovely day. To church twice. Played in the afternoon. Got on v. well. To the Iron Room with Kitty & Emily.

Morning Communion 40. 1st Girls 9

Afternoon Father 2 Corinthians XIII. 14

Evening Father Acts II. Edith had 20. Amos Catt there again.

Monday 6th

Lovely day. Heard from Dora. Did a quantity of bedding out – geraniums. A hamper of plants came from Johnnie B. – geraniums, violets, chrysanthemums, French Beans! & a pink. In the afternoon Father, Mother, Emily, Kitty & I drove to Bedgebury – in by Lovis Lodge & out near Flimwell. It all looked most lovely.

Tuesday 7th

Fine day. Went for a jolly ride at 10 45 with Mrs D'A to Benenden & home by Fox Hole. The lanes were all splendid with ferns & flowers. Helped Kitty pack.

Played croquet & then to see the Horsleys & in the shrubbery with them. Out after supper. Evelyn had the men to practise & showed them the bees after. Only Amos Catt, Hogben & J. Mallion.

Wednesday 8th

Lovely day. Father went up to the Lambeth Conference[49]. Kitty went away. Mrs Mallion came up to see us. Planted out some zinnias & poppies. To the village with Emily to see Mrs Gasson, Fancy Relf, Mrs J. Nash out, Mrs Vaughan, Mrs Judge & the Post Office. Came home by the fields. Most lovely. Mrs Horsley came into tea.

Thursday 9th

Lovely day. Sat out for an hour & read French with Emily & Evelyn. Darned stockings. Planted out some more geraniums. Drove to Highgate with Edith & the 2 little Horsleys. Evelyn for a ride & was out 3 hours! Mrs D'A & Mabel came here. Only Bobby came to the Band of Hope! To the Practice at 8. Got many there. Mr Horsley came.

Friday 10th

Lovely day again. The side passage was cleaned. Covered down some jam. Had a note from Kitty. Wrote to her & Dora Locock. Read French again. Stayed in the garden in the afternoon & put out some more plants. Jane to see me. Took her round the shrubbery. Father came home late.

Saturday 11th

Another lovely day. Marked out the tennis court. Evelyn went for a ride with Mabel at 10 30. Expected the Crofts & Matthews but they did not come. Johnnie Bryant sent a lovely basket of white azaleas for the church-yard. They revived & looked lovely. Planted geraniums & lobelias all round our darling's grave. Mr & Mrs Horsley to tea. – had some good games of tennis with him in the evening.

Sunday 12th

Lovely day. To church twice. Sat out under trees after church. Views lovely. Amos Catt's baby christened William Henry. Edith had 23!

Morning Mr Horsley 2 Corinthians IV. 5 I Girls 8

Afternoon Father Joshua XXIV. 13 Mr Horsley spoke to all the school.

Evening Mr Horsley I Samuel XII. 24

Went across the fields to the Iron Room.

Monday 13th

Splendid day. Intense heat. The bees swarmed twice. Took them & they went back both times. Put up an awning over them. Marked some Psalters. Mabel D'A came here & we went to Marsh Water Pond & got a quantity of iris roots. Walked part of the way with her.

Tuesday 14th

Glorious day. Again intensely hot. The bees swarmed before breakfast in 4 lots. Took them all & they all joined. Put them into the small box. Up to practise the organ. The white box swarmed. Searched for the Queen but did not find her. Most went back. Band of Hope at 6. 8 girls came. They went to sewing. Down to Old Place with Emily. Saw Mrs Catt & Jane & Mrs Mewitt & 2 children (Harriet Catt round the garden with Jane). Practice in evening.

Wednesday 15th

Splendid day again. Very hot still. The brown hive swarmed. Cox bought them for 5/-^{50}. Took them down to his house in the evening. Put some of yesterday's swarm into the newest spot. Miss Bell arrived at 1 15. Had a tea for the Y.W.C.A. members. 24 in all. Had tea on the lawn then Miss Bell spoke to us. Round the shrubbery with Jane & Lizzie. Meeting at Mission Room at 7. Several there. Miss Bell gave a nice address on John I. 49 & Mark I.17

Thursday 16th

Lovely day again. Wrote to Sarah. Had a Bible Reading at 12 o'c. The Horsleys came down. Very nice. Worked at some verses – Ezekiel XXXVI. 31, Jeremiah XXXI. 11-14, Exodus XIX. 14-16. Cox's bees swarmed. Lost & found them successfully!! Did some planting out. Meeting at the Iron Room for men & women at 8 o'c. Very good number there. Most striking address on Deuteronomy XXXII. 9-12. Enjoyed it v. much. Jesus seeking & finding. Jesus leading. Jesus teaching & Jesus keeping.

Friday 17th

Lovely day. Cooler. High East wind. Miss Bell left at 8 45. Read French in the morning. Took Etta & Anna for a walk to Marsh Water Wood. The others for a drive. Played tennis after tea. Mrs D' Aguila came. Settled to have a Missionary Box Tea![51]

Saturday 18th

Lovely day again. Read French in the morning. Up to the organ in the morning for an hour. Looked at the section boxes in the afternoon. None ready to take. Wrote to Maggie & Miss Hesse. Poor little Percy Nash drowned in the pump pond. Cox got him out after trying for an hour. He was playing here with Willie Verrall. Played tennis after tea. Father & Mother dined at the Hardcastles to meet the Bishop of Dover.

Sunday 19th

Lovely day. To church twice. Played in the afternoon. Read a good deal. Edith had 14.

Morning Father Luke XIV. 16 I Girls

Afternoon Father Acts III. II Boys. 10. Had them in the shrubbery. Very nice class. Stayed with Mother in the evening. Played some hymns in the evening.

Monday 20th

Lovely day. Bit colder wind. Began to correct the Home Study papers. 59 of one set! Then out in the garden. Planted out some salpiglossis & heliotrope. Evelyn went for a long ride. 3 hours. By Cripps Corner. Wrote the invitations for July 1st. Up to church & put round the Jubilee Hymns & Services[52].

Tuesday 21st

Most lovely day. Emily & Anne went down at 8 to help in the bread & butter. Had Service at 11. Very nice. Not v. many there. Father gave a nice little address on I Timothy II 1-2. Went down to see the dinner for all over 14 at 2 o'c. Nearly 500 people. All seemed happy. Then children had tea, pies, cake etc. in the tent. Then to Mr Cheeseman's field to watch the sports. Great fun stayed till 8 o'c (William got the leg of mutton). Went up the tower at 10. Mother with us!! To see the bonfires. Saw about 17 & several other glows. Mr Rice had one. Good ones at Silver Hill & Benenden.

Wednesday 22nd

Lovely day. Cold East wind. Emily & Edith went away to the Mildmay Conference[53]. Mary Ridout to stay here. Mother was about the accounts of yesterday's procession in London. Grand sight. All went off well. Marked tennis court. Looked at the bees. No honey quite ready. Played tennis in the evening. Mrs Horsley came down & we had some good sets. 8 little bantams hatched.

Thursday 23rd

Lovely day. To the organ in the morning. Had the Working Party in the afternoon. 5 came. Mother read to us all. Very interesting. Wrote to Leonard. Jane came round the garden with me. Played tennis again in the evening. Practice with Evelyn. Good many there. Went through the Anthem, Psalms & hymns.

Friday 24th

Fine day. To the organ at 10 30. Then to Old Place with Mary. Saw Mrs Catt. Then to Mrs Moss. Her hand is better. Saw Mr Neve. He took us round the garden & gave us some splendid roses. To the village in the afternoon to see Mrs Friar, Mrs Simes & Miss F. James & Miss Newman. Walked home with Jane. The others for a drive. Played tennis after tea. Heard from Maggie. Miss Harmer to stay here.

Saturday 25th

Dull day. To organ at 11. Practised the Psalms & corrected some more papers. Mrs Moore came up. Took her round the garden. She was charmed. Miss Thompson called. Evelyn & Mother to Field Green. Edith came home. Played tennis. Mrs Horsley came. Mrs Catt came up. Took her in the garden. Up to the church after supper. Did 3 tins of daisies & pinks. Primrose calved. The hay began.

Sunday 26th

Fine day. To church twice. Wrote to Emily. Went to the Iron Room with Mr Horsley.

Morning Mr Horsley Psalm CXXVI. 3   I Girls. 6. Had the Anthem 'O praise God' & Psalms

Afternoon Father I Peter II. 17 Mr Horsley spoke to all the children. Played in church – Psalms! & National Anthem.

Evening Mr Horsley. Hebrews II. 3 Edith had 15.

Monday 27th

Lovely day. The bees swarmed twice – found 2 Queens! But they did not go back. To the school to take the money. Then to see Mrs A. Field, Mrs Taylor, Mrs Jempson, Mrs R. Chantler & Mrs C. Willard. Worked in the hay in the afternoon. Heard that Charlie is going to leave Mortimer! So glad. Dear Primrose died. The calf all right.

Tuesday 28th

Lovely day. Worked hard in the hay all day. Began at 9 15 & went on until 7! Rather nervous at first. Father went to Tunbridge Wells for a clerical meeting. Heard from Uncle Arthur. Sophie left Alexandria.

Wednesday 29th

Lovely day again. Worked hard all day again. Got a good deal ready for carrying & thought up to 6 loads. Went in the pony carriage to meet Father at Highgate. Took Bobbie. Lovely evening. Sat out in the veranda until 9 30.

Thursday 30th

Dull day but fine. In the hay a good deal & got up 3 more loads. Heard from Emily. Corrected some more questions. Mrs D'A & Mrs Boyle came to tea. Up to the organ for a few minutes. Took the honey 1 ¼ lbs. To the Practice with Evelyn. Good many there. Had a long talk with Mrs Jempson.

JULY

Friday 1st

Lovely day. To the hay again – all day, working hard. Got up several more loads. The women did not come. Miss Goddard came to tea & up to the organ after. Emily came here. Sat out in a hay-cock. Mrs Bryant cut off the tips of her thumb. Very painful.

Saturday 2nd

Lovely day again. Finished the hay. They carried a good deal from the front. Intensely hot. Up to the organ afternoon & evening. Clara with me. Dear Charlie came home for the Sunday. Got here at 9 o'c looking very well. Mrs Bryant's hand still very painful.

Sunday 3rd

Glorious day but intensely hot. To school & church twice & to Iron Room in the evening.

Morning   Communion 42 I Girls 7

Afternoon   Father Luke XV. 3 II Boys 12

Evening   Father Acts X

Edith had 18. Well there!

Thermo. 107!![54]

Monday 4th

Lovely day again. Charlie went off at 8 40. To Old Place in the morning to see Mrs Moore & Mrs Bryant.

Worked at the bees & took a jar 4 ½ lbs! & 1 section seemed rather crowded. Corrected some more papers. Y.W.C.A. meeting. 11 there. Had it in the garden. Tied up some bunches for Edith. Sat out in the veranda until 9 45.

Tuesday 5th

Fine day. Rained a little in the morning. Corrected some more questions. Went for a ride with Cox to Northiam – got some beef for beef tea. Father not at all well. Very hoarse & seemed quite ill. Evelyn had notes from Arthur & May asking her to M/C.

Wednesday 6th

Lovely day. To the organ then picked some flowers & made 40 button holes. Cut the grass round all the borders. Then got the tables, seats, cups etc. ready. Had the Missionary Box Tea at 6 o'c. 30 came. Had tea on the lawn. Then round the garden shrubbery etc. Then played games. Then Mr Horsley spoke to them. They went at 9 o'c & all seemed happy.

Thursday 7th

Fine day. Very hot. Wrote to Miss Leff & did up my parcel. Down to the Summer House with Emily. About the garden with Evelyn & helped her pack. Picked a basket of strawberries to go to Arthur. To the Practice with Edith & played part of the time. Not many there. Sat out in the veranda later. The Gazette came. Lizzie Fellows commended.

Friday 8th

Lovely day. Very hot. Wrote to Dora. Father & Evelyn started for Newcastle at 6 45. To the organ in the morning. To the village in the afternoon. To see Lizzie Fellows, Mrs A. Catt, Mrs Judge, Miss Lowe & old Mrs Catt, who was in bed. Very ill. Read Mark 4 to her. Walked across the fields with Jane. Nice talk. Picked some strawberries for supper. Mrs Young came to see Mrs Bryant & did up her thumb.

Saturday 9th

Lovely day again. Did some Algebra with Emily. Then to the church with her. Round the shrubbery & down to see Cox's bantams. Heard from Sophie from Malta. For a drive in afternoon to see old R. Reeves. Read to him. Mother to Ethnam, Alderden & Field Green. To the organ after tea. Wrote to Emma.

Sunday 10th

Fine day. Misty later & fine rain. Looked out some more texts. Got some strawberries for supper.

Morning Mr Horsley Luke V. 8-11 | Girls 6.

Afternoon Mr Horsley Romans XII. 1 | Boys 10

Evening Mr Horsley Hebrews VII. Great High Priest

Edith had 16.

Monday 11th

Fine day. Picked strawberries in the morning. 13lbs. Then took Emily's dress down to Old Place. Drove Mother to the village to see Mrs Standen. Pony was v. lame. Dora Dodliet, Miss Andrews & Mrs Bendian called. Round the shrubbery with the 2 latter. Covered over some currant trees! Cox took a horse to the cattle field for Miss Bell.

Tuesday 12th

Lovely day. Did some Algebra & then looked at the bees & took 3lbs of honey. Sophie landed at Liverpool at about 3 o'c. In the afternoon to see Mrs G. Mallen then on with Emily to Hurst Wood. Had a tea picnic there with the Maynards. 15 in all. Mrs Horsley & the 2 children came. Played games after tea & went round the wood. Most lovely.

Wednesday 13th

Lovely day. Picked 7 lbs of gooseberries. Then began to arrange the prizes with Emily. Heard from Eunice. Had luncheon at 12 30. We had the carriage at 1 & went to the Hawkhurst Flower Show. Took all the Cox's. Tea at the Maynard's. It was held in their grounds. C. Willard got 7 prizes. & R. Hogben 8. Got home at 6. Found Father & dear Sophie looking very well & bright.

Thursday 14th

Lovely day. Cut out some work for the Working Party. Picked some strawberries for dessert. Out in the garden with Mother & Sophie. Had the Working Party at 2 30. 6 there. Alice Clarke new. Saw Jane for a few moments. Emily & Edith to the village. Edith had face-ache in the evening. To the Practice without her. Not many there.

Friday 15th

Fine day. Picked nearly 14 lbs of strawberries. It is for jam & got a few raspberries. Put up some flags to frighten the birds. Wrote some rose labels. Sophie's box arrived. Helped her unpack. Wrote to Evelyn. Jane

to see me in the evening. Had a nice talk & prayer with her. Lord, open our lips. Lent Jane 'Pilgrim's Progress'[55].

Saturday 16th

Lovely day. Covered down the strawberry jam & put it away. Took 1 section of honey. Packed up 6 lbs for Mrs Jull. Miss Goddard came up to see Sophie. Old Clark was buried. Up to the church. Ticked the books. Wrote the papers etc. Edith did 3 ties of roses. Saw Jane for a moment. John has asked her to go & keep his house. Advised her _not_ to go. Tied on some rose labels.

Sunday 17th

Fine early. Two heavy showers of rain in afternoon & in evening service. Ground much refreshed. Jane told me of John's engagement to Francis Hodkin!

Morning Father Mark VI 4-7

Afternoon Father. II Boys. I took them round the shrubbery & read to them in Summer House. Practice after.

Evening Father. Rain prayed for & it came![56]

Packed up in the evening a little & sang hymns.

Monday 18th

Lovely day. Left home with Father & Mother at 8 30. Drove to Staplehurst. Delicious drive. Train to Dover. Got several things at Metcalfs – pink dress, Norfolk jacket & white shoes. Had ½ an hour at Deal. Down to beach. 20 minutes at Sandwich. Mrs Jull & Mrs Godfrey arrived. Drove to Brook House, Ash. Found Mrs G. & 2 girls, Mabel & Kitty from Cheltenham. Unpacked & had some good games of tennis. Dinner at 7 45. Nice letter from Evelyn.

Tuesday 19th

Lovely day. Up at 7. Breakfast at 9. Walked to the village with Father to call on the Woods. & to see the church & old vicarage where Sophie & & El were born. Flower show in afternoon. About 100 people came. Mr Kirby here. Also, Mr & Mrs Laws Wilson (Nonnington), Mrs Plumptre & 9 daughters & Alice (Tredville) & a Mildmay Deaconess to whom I talked for some time. Also 3 Plumtres from Hunstanton. Talked of Kitty to them! Miss Knask to stay at home.

Wednesday 20th

Lovely day. Walked with Father & Mabel Godfrey to Conghurst to see Mr & Mrs Maylin. Nice people. For a drive in the afternoon to the church. Miss Gardner played the lovely organ to us. Then on to call on the Gardeners & Blakes where we had tea. Wrote to Evelyn & Edith.

Thursday 21st

Lovely day. Sat out in the garden in the morning working. Wrote to Charlie & Kitty. Practised in the afternoon. Walked to Richborough with Father & Mother. Pretty old ruins. Nice walk by the fields. Played some duets with Mother.

Friday 22nd

Lovely, very hot day. Left Ash at 11. Came by Minster, Canterbury & Ashford to Rye where Cox met us. Nice letter from Dora. Dusty drive. Got home at 3 30. Found Miss Brunskill here – all well. Sat out under the trees. Unpacked & & put my room a little straight.

Saturday 23rd

Fine day. Looked at the bees in the morning. No sections ready. Up to the church with Sophie. Marked the books, wrote the papers etc. Down to Old Place with Emily to see Mrs W. Burt. Ernie pinched his finger in a machine very badly. Saw Jane for a moment. The Maynards & Miss King came to tea. Picked cherries & strawberries for supper.

Sunday 24th

Lovely day. To church & Sunday School twice. Iron Room. Edith had 27!

Morning Mr Horsley Mark VIII. I Girls 8

Afternoon Father Psalms CXVI. 1-2

Evening Mrs Brunskill Luke XIX. 42-44 Thy day, peace, visitation. Solemn.

Monday 25th

Lovely day. Helped Edith arrange the Mission Room. Find games etc. The men came at 6 o'c. Showed Amos Catt the bees, honey, sections. Then they played bowls, rounders, leap frog until 7 30. Tea in the Mission Room. 26. Very full. Then round the shrubbery once & back to the Mission Room. Games. Microscope. Much excited over it! Miss Brunskill spoke to them at end about witnessing. 'Go home to thy friends'[57]. Left at 10 30. All v. happy.

Tuesday 26th

Fine day. Had face ache all day & part of night. The Horsleys came down and we had a little Bible Reading. Picked 15lbs of redcurrants & staged them. To the village with Emily to see Mrs Taylor. Well! Mrs Collins with her. Then to Mrs Simes, Mrs Judge & Mrs Vaughan – out. To bed early. Marked several choir books.

Wednesday 27th

Fine day. My face all right again. Heard from Eva Locock of the serious illness of their father. Wrote to her. Marked some more choir books & began to cover down the jam. Walked up to Downgate – Hodgkins out. Saw Mrs Pope. Miss Brunskill spoke at Iron Room in evening. About 50 there. Beautiful address on Hebrews IX & the appearings Past, Present & Future.

Thursday 28th

Lovely day. Very hot. Covered down a quantity of jam & put up some new shelves in the storeroom. Tea after. The others drove to 'Baby Castle'. Had the Working Party & besides Clara, Mary, Mrs Field, Mrs Cox & Jane & Elizabeth Catt attendance 9 - Mrs Bryant, Mrs A. Clark. Down to Cowgate with Jane. Saw Mrs Job Catt. Heard better account of Sir C. Locock. Mildred taken ill with typhoid fever[58].

Friday 29th

Fine morning. Wet later. Helped Sophie tidy her cupboard. Then showed her the prizes. To the village with Emily to see Mrs A. Burt. Saw her for a moment. Then to P. Milton, Mrs Piper. Nice talk with her. Then joined Emily at Miss Barley & home with her. Evelyn & Leonard home in the evening. Helped Evelyn unpack & tidy own room.

Saturday 30th

Lovely day. Round the garden with Evelyn & Leonard. Edith & I painted the iron work of darling's grave. Looked so nice. Very hot work. To the organ with Sophie in afternoon. Wrote papers etc. Edith & Miss Brunskill to see Mrs W. Slaughter, Mrs Robards & Mrs Catt. A. Burt came up to see me in the evening. Very nice talk with him. Still seeking but can't say 'My Saviour'[59]. Miss Brunskill talked to him & I do believe he will soon come in.

Sunday 31st

Lovely day. To church twice. Practice after afternoon service. G. Head & D. Catt came to tea. The latter came back into the choir.

Morning Father Luke XI. 27-28 I Girls 10.

Afternoon Father Phil. I. 9-10. Miss Brunskill spoke to the school.

Evening Miss Brunskill Acts XXVI. 18. Job Catt there.

Edith had 26.

Dear Mildred Carter died at 2am.

AUGUST

Monday 1st

Lovely day. Looked at the bees with Evelyn. Took 2 sections. In the afternoon, drove with Edith, Miss Brunskill & Evelyn to Highgate & on to the Springfield's where the others called. Sat out in the evening & worked at my cap. Mrs Horsley, Ella & Anna came to tea. Picked fruit for supper.

Tuesday 2nd

Lovely day. Miss Brunskill went away to meet the omnibus. Very hot day. Went through the prizes again & Evelyn wrote in a few names. Charlie came home in the evening by the last train. Leonard met him. To the village with Edith to see Mrs Taylor. Mrs A. Burt, Mrs Vaughan, Mrs Newman, Mrs Seney & Mrs Page. Got some carnations.

Wednesday 3rd

Lovely day. Charlie told Evelyn & me of his engagement to Miss Lilla Smith. He was much brighter & seemed much happier. He stays on at Mortimer. Picked currants. Very much shocked to see darling Mildred's death in the Times. Wrote to Mabel Carter, Marian & Dora Locock. The D'As to tea. Did not see them.

Thursday 4th

Lovely day. Up early. Charlie, Evelyn, Leonard, Mabel D'A & I drove to Staplehurst & on to Canterbury for the day. Charlie left us at Ashford. He joins Pablo at Folkestone & on to Paris. We got to Canterbury about 11 & went over the Cathedral first. Streets looked very bright & pretty. Then on to the cricket field. Had a picnic luncheon & watched the cricket – Kent V Middlesex till 3 30. Then found Mr & Mrs Godfrey & the Freemantles at home where we had tea. Dinner at 10.

Friday 5th

Lovely day. Rested in the morning then finished the prizes. Clara gave us 3 dolls. Service at 2 at church. Father spoke on Proverbs VIII.17. 162 children & several women came also. D'As, Marches, Oakes, Mills, Mrs Neve, Mrs Spodridge. Played the usual games & ball with the small boys. Made great friend with Leonard. We all congratulated her she seemed v. happy. Tea at 4. Prizes given at 5. I then played on till 8. Up the shrubbery with Jane.

Saturday 6th

Lovely day. Heard from Dora & Marian all about dear Mildred's death. So sudden & unexpected. Funeral at 4 o'c on Thursday. Picked some cherries for a tart. Knitted a good deal of my cape. Intensely hot all day. Sophie, Evelyn & I to the French's garden party. Did the flowers in churchyard. Saw Jane there. Nice talk with her.

Sunday 7th

Lovely day. To church & Sunday School twice. Practice after afternoon service. Copied some hymns & wrote out 'Sleep' for Marion.

Morning Communion 60 I Girls 10

Afternoon Mr Horsley II Corinthians X. 13 II Boys 12

Evening Father John XV. 1-2

Edith had 20.

Monday 8th

Lovely day. Evelyn & I looked at the bees. We both got stung. My finger swelled up very much. Edith arranged the tables etc. on the lawn. Had the Mothers' Meeting Tea at 4 0'c & 23 came. After tea played games – bat & ball etc. Then round the shrubbery. They stayed till past 8. Mrs Bryant hurt her eye! Mrs Amos Catt brought her baby which Clara took care of.

Tuesday 9th

Fine day. My finger still very much swollen & hurt a good deal. Sat out in the garden part of the day. Mrs Simes to tea. Read 'Preston Fight'[60]. Read to the servants for a few minutes. Miss Lawe came up to say goodbye. She goes to Mrs Parker as servant. Heard from Lovedy.

Wednesday 10th

My finger & hand still very much swelled. Got out a little bit of the sting. Father, Mother, Sophie, Evelyn & Leonard to tea at Field Green. Had tea early. Went by the fields to see Francis Hodgkins – stayed some three hours – quite charmed with her. Did all the watering in the garden later. The Horsleys came down to see us. Cut up pictures for Scrap Books.

Thursday 11th

Fine day. Helped Sophie mark the tennis ground. Read French & did some Algebra with Emily. Had the Working Party. Only 3 besides Clara & May. Colonel & Mrs D'A, Mabel & Mattie Parnell came to tea. Had a good game of tennis after. Wrote to May Robinson.

Friday 12th

Lovely day. Mother, Emily Leonard & I went over to Tunbridge Wells for the Agricultural Show. Went by the 11 19. Saw lovely cows & horses. Left at 5 28 - too early! The riding & jumping was most exciting. Cox & Bryant went also. Some good poultry & rabbits. Bought a few things at Goldsmiths. Met Charlie Brown Douglas at Etchingham. Nice drive home. Got in at 6 30. Very hungry. Played Mattadore in the evening.

Saturday 13th

Lovely day. Picked some currants & cherries. Had a most exciting game of croquet. Emily & I & Evelyn & Charlie Brown Douglas. In the afternoon Emily, Edith, Evelyn & Charlie Brown Douglas drove round by Benenden & Rolvenden. Lovely drive. To see Rolvenden church. Played tennis after tea. To the church with Edith. The Horsleys dined here. Played Mattadore & the 'blowing' game which Charlie Brown Douglas taught us. He sang to us & we had some glees[61].

Sunday 14th

Lovely day. To church & Sunday School twice & to Iron Room in evening. Edith had 27. Sang hymns & anthems till 10 o'c. The others to Bodiam Castle.

Morning Mr Horsley Phil IV. 6-7

Afternoon Mr Horsley Luke XI. 31-32

Charlie Brown Douglas spoke to the children in the afternoon on Psalm CXIX – What, where, why, whom. <u>Very</u> nice, indeed.

Monday 15th

Lovely day. Had another very good game of croquet – Emily & I, Evelyn & C.B.D. he went away at 11. Down to Old Place with Leonard. Nice talk with Jane & Mrs Catt. Looked at the bees with Evelyn. Took 11lbs of honey, making 55lbs this year. Tea early. Walked to the village with Sophie by the fields. I to see Mrs Head. Very ill. Then to Mrs Judge & Mrs A. Fields. Sorry to miss the Y.W.C.A. class. 13 at it. Wrote to Dora & Marion. Helped Sophie paste some books.

Tuesday 16th

Showery day. Leonard for a ride before breakfast & he got quite wet! Heard from May Robinson. Read French & helped Evelyn tear up some paper. Then tidied my box. Played croquet. Drove to the village with Father & Sophie. Did not go to see anyone. Played Mattadore with Evelyn.

Wednesday 17th

Heavy rain in the night & it continued showery all day. More than which altogether very thankful for it. Leonard left at 6 45 to go by sea to Newcastle! Caught a good deal of water in the baths. Read French & did some Algebra & practised. The large 'Madonna' picture came down! Wrote to Lovedy. Tidied some of my drawers & helped Sophie look through some books.

Thursday 18th

Fine day. Heard from Kitty & Dora. Read French. Picked some currants. Father, Mother, Sophie & Emily drove to Benenden & called on Canon Joy. Evelyn & I walked to the village. To see Mrs Head, A. Catt, Job Catt, School etc. Took the Choir Tea invitations. Heard that Harry Piper has pleurisy. Sent him some linseed[62]. Played croquet.

Friday 19th

Showery day. Picked 12 lbs of currants for preserving. Heard of Leonard's arrival. Read French. Received some choir books. Father, Mother, Sophie & Evelyn to the School Treat. Edith & I to Ethnam to see Mrs W. Slaughter. Nice walk. Had a nasty cold. Very hoarse. Worked at Mother's cape. Up at 5 & saw the eclipse of the sun. Well!

Saturday 20th

Fine early. A most fearful thunderstorm came up from North East at 10 30. Heavy rain & vivid lightning. One truly awful crash when the acacia mountain ash &

yellow holly trees were struck! Marvellous presentation, for we were all that side of the house. Covered down some jam & helped Evelyn with honey later. Mother, Sophie, Emily & Evelyn to the garden party at Downgate. Harvey Piper still very ill. Also, old Marshall. Up to church with Edith. Did the books.

Sunday 21st

Lovely day. To church & Sunday School twice. Had 11 boys in afternoon. Did a clock with them as I was very hoarse. Up the shrubbery with Jane.

Morning Mr Horsley Psalm CVI. 23 I Girls 11

Evening Father Psalm XCII. 1-3

Changed the service to 6 30 instead of afternoon & evening. Great many people at church. Edith had her class at the Iron room at 2 30. She had 26. William Goode & Tom Winer!

Monday 22nd

Lovely day. Father & Mother went away early. They go to York for Constance's wedding. Read some French etc. Sophie, Edith & I went to village. Emily & I played croquet then down to Old Place. Saw Jane alone. She told me her secret. Miss Elsam came to tea. Played croquet with her. Later Leonard Willard came up & signed Band of Hope again.

Tuesday 23rd

Lovely day. Constance Daniells was married to Mr Graves in York Minster. Father, Mother, Arthur, May, Sarah & Leonard were here & say it was a lovely sight.

Sophie, Emily, Edith & I to garden party at the Springetts. Not very exciting. Got back at 6 30. Evelyn heard from Charles. Miss Bushnell to luncheon from Downgate.

Wednesday 24th

Lovely day. Read French & did some Algebra in the morning. Father, Mother & Leonard came home in the evening. Had the Working Party. 4 there. Nice talk with Jane after. Sophie, Emily & Evelyn to Field Green. The little Horsleys to tea. Played croquet with them. Charlie & Pablo duly arrived home at 10 15. They walked from Staplehurst.

Thursday 25th

Lovely day. Sat out under the trees in the morning. Had the Choir Treat. They came at 2 30 & had cricket in upper field which we watched. The boys had tea in the garden at 5 20. Then the men dined in hall at 6 30. Charlie, Mr & Mrs Horsley & Pablo dined with them. Then to Mission Room & they played games till 10 20. All seemed very happy.

Friday 26th

Fine early. Heard from Dora. Played croquet with Pablo & Emily & Leonard. Pablo & I to the Fothergills' garden party. Went round the garden & examined the curiosities with Pablo. It came on to rain so we came away early. Charlie & Evelyn to Field Green. Fred Terby to stay here. He is not a bit altered since 1880. But looking very ill[63]. Has been out in Burmah[64].

With her father's love

Saturday 27th

Wet early. Fine later. Edith went away to Cromer to stay with Evelyn Smith. Charlie to station with her. In the afternoon, Evelyn, Charlie, Leonard, Fred, Pablo & I walked to Bodiam Castle & on to the wharf & to see the Jubilee Hall. Pablo & Leonard to the Belchers. Nice walk. To the church after tea. Wrote to May. Mother walked to see Mrs Harmer & sprained her left leg. Very lame, indeed.

Sunday 28th

Showery day. To church twice & Sunday School. Went for a walk in afternoon with Charlie. Leonard, Fred, Pablo & Evelyn down to acre & up through the wood. Bad hops. Had some nice singing in the evening. Went on till 10 15.

Morning Father I Kings XXII I Girls only 5

Afternoon Took 1st Boys at Sunday School. 10 there. Miss Elsam came to teach

Evening Father. Mark VII. 37

Sophie took Edith's class & had 20. Mother not out all day.

Monday 29th

Showery day. Out in the garden with Fred. Then Emily, Charlie, Leonard, Evelyn, Fred, Pablo & I walked to the village to see Mrs Vaughan for a moment. In the afternoon, Charlie, Leonard, Evelyn & Fred to the garden party at Boazels. About with Pablo. We played bagatelle. Then out & up to the organ. Played Squails[65] in the evening. To bed late. Jane & F. Hodgkin to see me.

Tuesday 30th

Showery day. Heard from Miss Brunskill. Wrote to her. Evelyn & Fred to see Mrs Harmer. Then had a game of croquet. Leonard out down the 'smelly tree' to try & find some bugs for Pablo but did not find any. Lionel to luncheon. About the garden etc with the two boys. Gave Pablo a sun-flower for his button-hole! Played card games in the evening.

Wednesday 31st

Showery again. Helped Fred pack up. The two boys went off at 11 15. Fred to Monks Orchard & Pablo home. Very sorry to lose them. Missed them v. much. Heard from Edith. Wrote to her & Kitty. Up to see F. Hodgkin with Sophie. Saw her nice presents. Gave her 'Daily Light'[66]. Father, Emily & Leonard to garden party at the Belchers. Mother, Sophie & Charlie to Field Green. Evelyn & I tidied up. Finished Mother's cape.

With her father's love

SEPTEMBER

Thursday 1st

Very stormy day. Leonard to shoot over Old Place with Mr Carter. He got 12 brace of partridges & 5 hares. F. Hodgkin to see Mother. Tidied up own room. Helped Sophie alter her room. Charlie & Evelyn for a ride with Leonard by Cripps Corner. Emily & I to the village to see Gasson. Mr Heath from Open Air Museum came here for hoppers.

Friday 2nd

Very stormy & a regular gale blowing all day. Not out at all in the morning. Cut out 2 shirts & began to make one of them. Out to pick up apples & pears later. Up to the church in the afternoon. Marked some books. The others mending the organ. Lionel came to tea & Charlie & Leonard rode with him. Several large boughs came down in the shrubbery.

Saturday 3rd

Still windy. Up to church with Emily & Evelyn. Marked some books & pumped the organ. Walked to the Elsams in the afternoon. Saw Mrs Elsam. Then on the farm with Mr Elsam & went over his oast. Charlie rode to Risden & Field Green & dined at the latter. Played games in the evening & worked at my shirt.

Sunday 4th

Stormy day. To church twice & Sunday School. Miss Elsam came to the Open Air Service & stayed to tea. Had Practice at 6. Mrs Neve to dinner.

Morning   Singing at Sunday School

Afternoon   Sunday School. Mr Horsley spoke. Open Air Service on Green at 3 30. Mr Heath spoke. Nearly 200 people.

Evening   Mr Horsley 2 Kings VI. 33.

Sophie had 12. Charlie & Leonard for a walk with Lionel & Mabel.

Monday 5th

Showery day. Read some French. The wool came from Jevons. Began a Fisherman's Stocking. Mabel & Lionel came in afternoon. The latter ferreted with Charlie & Leonard. & got 4 rabbits. They stayed to dinner & we had the 'blowing game'. Jane to see me in the evening. Had a very nice talk with her. Heard all arrangements for tomorrow.

Tuesday 6th

Showery day. We all went up to church at 11 to see John Catt & Francis Hodgkin married. 4 bridesmaids Jane, Ada, Miss Newburn & a friend. Mrs Jempson & Mrs Taylor came & 5 boys. Had 2 hymns 'The voice that breathed' & 'How welcome'[67]. Sophie took 2 photos but both on same plate! Pity. Charlie, Leonard & Lionel for a ride. Went in Mr T. Collins' hop garden to help. Mrs A. Burt, Mrs Simes, Mrs Vaughan, Mrs Gasson, Mrs A. Catt, Mrs Judge, Mrs Hodge & Mrs Wickens, Sophie & Emily went with me. Leonard to the Downs' tennis party. The happy pair to London. Bertie Ridout came here.

Wednesday 7th

Showery day. Charlie went away. Mother & Sophie to Etchingham with him. Leonard took Bertie to Major Fothergill's for tennis. About the garden in the afternoon. Worked at my enormous stocking. Jane came in & brought me a piece of excellent wedding cake!

Thursday 8th

Lovely day. Cox went for his holiday. George Vaughan to do the stable work. Leonard & I went for a v. jolly ride to Highgate & round by the Hardcastles. Most lovely morning. Mr & Mrs & Miss Mullens to luncheon. They went to the church. View most perfect. Leonard & Bertie to tennis at the French's. To Field Green. Sophie & Emily to Mrs Greenhill's. Kit Fanshawe to stay here. Wrote to Edith, Dora & Fred.

Friday 9th

Lovely day. Down to Old Place – to hop garden. There to oast where we weighed in. Emily, Evelyn, Kit, Mabel D'A, Leonard, Bertie & I were taken round the garden. Lionel to luncheon. Took the little Horsleys to Alderden hop garden. Helped Mrs Goode, Mrs Mallion, Mrs Hodgkins, Mr Booth etc. The others to Mrs Rollin's garden party.

Saturday 10th

Fine day. Very cold. Leonard was not well in the morning. In the afternoon, he & I to Old Place & we took a group of Mrs Catt, Mrs Hodgkins, Jane & Ada. V. good. Developed them in the evening. Then Evelyn,

Kit & Sophie to the Hardcastles for tennis. Sophie & I tried to mend the Mission Room harmonium. Then up to the church. Did the flowers & practised the organ. Arthur & May left. Edith to Woodhall with Evelyn Smith.

Sunday 11th

Fine day. To church & Sunday School twice. Sophie had 17 at her class. Leonard printed one or 2 photos. V. good. Heard from Margaret.

Morning   Father 2 Kings X. 16. Played for Sunday School singing.

Afternoon Sunday School I Boys. Open Air Service near the Wheelwright's. Emily, Evelyn, Kit & I went. Mr Heath spoke. V. nice. To the Practice with Sophie.

Evening   Father. Luke XVII. 17. Leonard read the lesson both times.

Monday 12th

Lovely day. Leonard took Kit for a ride to Staplecross. Sophie, Emily & I to luncheon with the Hardcastles. Only Evelyn, Kate, Beatrice, Leonard & Marjory at home. Saw over part of the house & then explored the garden. Lovely flowers. To see the chickens etc & stable & kitchen garden! Arthur & May arrived about 7. So nice to have them again.

Tuesday 13th

Fine day. V. cold. We started out at 10 15. Father, Arthur, May, Emily, Kit, Leonard & I for Bodiam. Leonard & I by Old Place. Found the 2 boats. Emily, Leonard & I in small one. We sailed beautifully part of

With her father's love

the way as far as Wittersham. Bought loaf at Newenden. Had luncheon on bank. I went up to see the church at Witttersham. Towed both boats back all the way. Took turns. Walked up with Kit & Leonard. Found Edith home & Charlie arrived later. Played games. To bed late. V. tired.

Wednesday 14th

Fine day. Helped Leonard pack & Edith unpack! Leonard took a group of us all which Charlie & I developed in the evening. Dear Leonard went off at 1 15. Charlie to the station with him. Arthur rode to Field Green. Edith & I walked to Silverden Lane. Found Mrs Harmer died yesterday. To see Mrs Osborne. About the garden in evening. Charlie showed his room etc to Kit. He & Arthur sang in the evening. Kit packed & we carried down her boxes. Not in bed till after 12.

Thursday 15th

Fine day. Kit went off at 10 15. Arthur to Etchingham station with her. Printed some photos. Picked some v. curious. We all went down to the Old Place Oast & saw it all over. Wrote to Leonard. The others played croquet. Charlie picked the pears. Played Patience. Saw Jane for a moment.

Friday 16th

Very showery day. Did not go out much. Arthur made a curious machine for drawing figures. Helped him in the morning. Worked at my shirt a good deal. Lionel & Mabel came in for a few minutes in the evening. Played Patience with Arthur. Charlie & I developed the first group. It was very good of some.

Saturday 17th

Very showery again. Not out in the morning. Charlie went for a ride & got very wet. Mother, Arthur, May & Evelyn to tea at Field Green. Up to the church with Emily. Arranged the books & did the flowers. Cox came back again. He was mercifully preserved from being in an awful railway accident at Doncaster yesterday[68].

Sunday 18th

Lovely day. V. cold. To church & Sunday School twice. Edith had 17. Down to the Summer House before tea. Mr & Mrs Horsley to tea.

Morning Father. Played for the Sunday School singing.

Afternoon Had II Boys.

Evening Mr Horsley. To the Practice with Sophie & Evelyn.

Monday 19th

Fine day. Arthur & May left us at 8 30. Picked them some violets. In the afternoon Charlie, Evelyn, & I drove to Highgate in pony carriage. To Williams etc. Charlie called at Risden & then we went to tea at Field Green & stayed till 6 30. Quite cold driving home. Played Patience in the evening.

Tuesday 20th

Lovely day. Picked some currants. Charlie & Evelyn took one hive. 15 lbs of honey. They went for a ride in the afternoon. I drove Sophie & Emily to the village & Lower End. Saw Mrs Christmas for a moment. Charlie printed some vignette photos & mounted them.

Wednesday 21st

Fine day. Picked some violets for Charlie. I went to the station with him. He drove the pair! Evelyn & I picked the mulberries & a few blackberries. Found A. Lockyer & Osborne taking mushrooms! Sent Cox after them. Read French after tea. Wrote to Pablo.

Thursday 22nd

Lovely day. Read French. The drawing-room chimney swept. In the afternoon Evelyn & I found Mabel at Downgate & explored Mr French's wood. So lovely. Got some blackberries & roots of heather. On to tea at Field Green where we found Emily & Edith all home together. Nice letter from Mabel Carter. To the Practice with Sophie. 8 men. 7 boys. V. good practice.

Friday 23rd

Lovely day. Heard from Margaret Locock. Practised piano & singing. Then read French. Picked some violets for Clara. She went for her holiday. Mother, Sophie & Evelyn for a drive. I drove Father to the village & Sponden. Finished my 2nd huge stocking. Up to the church with Sophie after tea.

Saturday 24th

Lovely day. Heard from Pablo. Wrote to Emma Emery & Frances Catt! Sent her one photo of each group. Heard from Leonard, too, sending me some photos. Went for a jolly ride at 2 o'c with Cox by Brick Kilns Junction & home by Bodiam. Very nice. Mrs Neve finished hopping.

Sunday 25th

Fine day. Sophie was not well & stayed in bed all day. Evelyn played for the Psalms.

Morning 1st Girls. Father Luke VII.

Afternoon II Boys. Father.

Evening To the Iron Room again. Mr Penfold spoke on Matthew XIV.

Monday 26th

Fine day. Heard from Fred at <u>last</u>. To the village with Emily in the afternoon. Took some of the Harvest notices. To see Mrs Judge, Mrs Simes & Mrs A. Catt. It rained a little & so I came home. Evelyn had face-ache. Mother, Sophie & Edith to Field Green. Jane to see me in the evening. Father went away to Charlton.

Tuesday 27th

Fine day. Wrote to Eva & Maggie. It was showery in the afternoon. Walked to see Mrs G. Mallion. V. nice talk with her. Told me about James. Had the Band of Hope for the Girls. 7 came. P. Rill was a new one. Worked at my shirt in the evening. Practised & read French. Also did some Algebra.

Wednesday 28th

Fine day. Wrote to Ann Brazier. Practised. Read French & did Algebra. Then out in the garden. Had the Band of Hope for Boys. 6 there. Bertie Simes stayed to tea. Edith had her 1st Boys Class. I had 20!

Thursday 29th

Fine day. Heard from Margaret Lovedy. About the garden in morning. Picked some violets which Evelyn sent to Pablo. In the afternoon, Mother, Sophie, Edith & I drove to Mountfield. Lovely drive. The Crofts were out. Called on the Loosemores. Out. To Practice with Sophie. Nearly all there. Wrote to Kitty.

Friday 30th

Fine day. Heard from Miss Legg. To the village with Sophie & Emily. I took several notices of Monday & Harvest. To Mrs Cheeseman, Miss Taylor, Mrs Gasson, Miss Bontemps, Mrs Chantler, G. Fellows, F. Relf, Mrs Vaughan. Verrall out. Mrs Friar, A. Field, Job Catt & M. Milton. Had the Boys to practise at the Mission Room in the evening.

OCTOBER

Saturday 1ˢᵗ

Fine day. Wrote to Leonard & Uncle Arthur. In the garden in the morning. Edith picked apples. Did some gardening with Evelyn. Moved some Pinks & Forget me nots. Up to the church with Edith. Prepared a lesson on Jacob with Evelyn. The Horsleys & Chandler came to supper.

Sunday 2ⁿᵈ

Fine day. To church twice. Walked up to Downgate with the D'A's. In the garden with Evelyn after tea.

Morning 1ˢᵗ Girls. Only 6. Communion 59. Nice number.

Afternoon Mr Chandler spoke to the children. Mr Horsley Isaiah LX. 1-3.

Evening To the Iron Room. Mr Maynard gave a nice address on the 4 burdens – 1 of circumstances, 2 of self, 3 of sin & 4 of Saviour. Walked home with Jane.

Monday 3ʳᵈ

Fine day. The Horsleys went away. Mr Barnes arrived at 10 o'c. He shewed us some photos. He spoke to the School at 3 45 & had a meeting at the Iron Room at 7. Room crammed. Over 300. Most interesting lecture on Egypt, Soldiers & Holy Land[69]. He dressed up 4 girls, Hodgkin & 2 children! Mrs Rolley, the Hardcastles & the Selmes came. Sent violets to Dora & Charlie. Wrote to them & Marion.

With her father's love

Tuesday 4th

Fine day. Mr Barnes went away early. Evelyn & I drove to Field Green in the afternoon. Found Mabel was not well so we did not stay. Went blackberrying in our fields & Mrs Neve with May. Got 6 ¾ lbs. Splendid ones. Evelyn & I had the 'Young Men' for extra practice.

Wednesday 5th

Fine day. Went blackberrying for an hour again. Got 9 ½ lbs more which was all made into jam. Sophie & Emily lunched at Collingwood. Evelyn for a ride. To the village with Edith. Took Mrs Friar some flowers & to see Mrs P. Milton & Mrs Taylor. Also to the School. Had the Girls Band of Hope. Only 7. Sophie took the Bible Class & had 19.

Thursday 6th

Fine day. Very cold. Edith to the village & the others for a drive. Had the Working Party. Only 5. Nice talk with Jane. To the Practice in the evening. Nearly all there. Went through the Harvest hymns & anthem.

Friday 7th

Fine day. Sang in the morning. Then did some text work 'Fear not, O Land. For the Lord will do great things'[70]. Edith & I went in the pony carriage to the Maynards & brought Clara back. Mabel D'A came in afternoon. We went blackberrying. Got 6 lbs. Evelyn, Kate Hardcastle & Mrs Hardcastle & the Bishop came to tea. Did not stay long. Took them round the garden. Wrote to Miss Legge & Miss Lovedy.

Saturday 8th

Fine day. Practised in the morning. To the church & finished putting the letters on the text. In the afternoon to Mrs Popes and Downgate with Emily. Gave Willie 2 shirts. Saw Mrs Manville. Picked a quantity more walnuts. Charlie Brown Douglas arrived at 7. Quite cold in the evening.

Sunday 9th

Fine day. To church twice. Charlie Brown-Douglas took Evelyn's class & went for a walk in the afternoon. Sang hymns in the evening.

Morning I Girls 7. Father Phil. III. 9

Afternoon II Boys 10. Father.

Evening Mr Everett – he spoke on 2 Samuel IX. Mephibosheth. Rather disappointed. Pitched about right.

Monday 10th

Showery day. Wrote to Fred, Pablo & Selina. In the morning up to church with Evelyn. Put on a good deal of the border of the text. Very wet afternoon. Worked & read 'Cranford'[71] a good deal. Had some singing in the evening. Did not go to bed till late. After tea Evelyn & I walked with C.B.D. to the village & back by Downgate. Rained part of the time.

Tuesday 11th

Fine day. Very cold. Edith & Charlie walked to Ethnam. Finished the border of the text. Mother, Evelyn, Emily & Charlie for a drive. To the Y.W.C.A. Meeting with

Edith. 13 there. She talked about Joseph. Played croquet in the evening. Bitterly cold! Then to Practice. Good many there.

Wednesday 12th

Snowed hard from 6 – 7 30. Thermo 26 degrees[72]. To church at 9 30 & up there till 1. Jane came & helped us & Charlie was also up. It looked pretty. Evelyn, Edith & Charlie to Field Green. Mrs Sherbrooke arrived at 5 30. Dinner at 6. Service at 7. Church full. Over 300. Singing very nice. Anthem 'Thou crownest'. Grand sermon on Jeremiah V.24. So nice. Mr Simes spoke later. Sat up in church room talking till 11 15! Then finished with prayers.

Thursday 13th

Fine day. Thermo. 22 degrees. Evelyn & I went in the wagonette to the station with Mrs Sherbrooke & Charlie. They went off by 9 30 train. Walked up Bodiam Hill with Mr Sherbrooke. He spoke of witnessing by our lives. In the afternoon, Emily, Evelyn & I walked to Mrs Rollings for Deep Sea Mariners' Meeting[73]. Mr Mather, G. Maynard & 2 skippers spoke. Very interesting. The Frenchs brought Eve. Walked from there. Edith had 21.

Friday 14th

Showery day. Frost again. Minnie went away. Worked at my shirts. Practised. In the afternoon to the village with Emily & Edith to see Mrs Judge, A. Burt out, P. Milton & A. Milton-Piper. Put off the Band of Hope as it was wet. Cox clipped the pony & big horse. To the

Practice with Evelyn. Not very many there. Practised Psalms & some fresh hymns. Very cold evening.

Saturday 15th

Lovely day but bitterly cold. North East Wind. In the garden in the morning. Picked some more walnuts. Cox clipped the little horse & saw they wanted exercise so he & I rode at 3 o'c. The big one went most beautifully. Went by the Junction, Cripps Corner, Staplecross & Bodiam. Out 2 ½ hours. Enjoyed it immensely. Read.

Sunday 16th

Lovely day. To church twice. Copied some nice bits out of Atty Smith's book which Charlie left us. Wrote to Leonard.

Morning I Girls 7. Father. I Thessalonians I. 1-3

Afternoon II Boys 10. Father. Ephesians IV.1

Evening George Maynard gave a beautiful address on Mephibosheth! People were most attentive.

Monday 17th

Lovely day, though cold. Finished 2nd shirt. In the garden from 12 & picked some violets for Anne who went for her holiday. Heard from Lovedy sending me a pretty handkerchief. Talked to Albert Catt & to Mrs Mann, Mrs Page & Mrs Gasson. Boys Band of Hope. 13 came! 5 new ones. 2 Wickens. H. Mills, S. Nash & A.E. Moore. Got in at 5 30. W. Catt came up. Gave him 1 shirt. Talked to him about a night school.

Tuesday 18th

Dull day. Out in the garden with Mother in the morning. Ava calved a dear little calf & she seemed going on well. Down to Old Place in the afternoon to see Mrs Moore & the Catts. Got in at 4. Had a card from Miss Hesse telling me of a parcel.

Wednesday 19th[74]

Lovely day. Had 10 letters! Some lovely presents. My watch from Father & Mother – a great beauty. Had £50[75] from Aunt L's legacy. Poor dear Ava very ill all day & died about 9 o'c. Very sad. A most exciting parcel from 'Bournemouth' containing a lovely silver pencil case from Anne, Clara & Jane. Down to Old Place with Sophie to see Mrs Cox with Mother. Wrote to Miss Hesse & Anne. Had a nice cake. Helped Mother & Sophie pack up.

Thursday 20th

Cold day. Mother & Sophie went away at 8 30. Cut some work for this afternoon. Had 8 at the Working Party. Shewed Jane my presents. Heard from Uncle Arthur. Wrote to Arthur. Emily & Evelyn to Field Green. To the Practice with Evelyn. Only Mrs Taylor & most of the boys. Gave W. Catt the other shirt.

Friday 21st

Fine day. Wrote to Leonard & Eunice. Swept up some leaves. In the afternoon drove Father to the Lower End. Then stayed in the village to see Mrs Vaughan. & Mrs G. Mallion. Had her own notes of the 12th inst. talk.

Promised her a petticoat. Began May's white cape. Mother & Sophie to the Hesses.

Saturday 22nd

Lovely day. Evelyn for a ride by Northiam & Ewhurst. Got up some violet plants for Aunt M. Helped Evelyn to get her things together. Helped Nellie Cox begin a pair of mittens. Up to the church later. Cut the grass on darling's grave. Prepared a lesson on Numbers VI. Wrote the Choir papers etc.

Sunday 23rd

Lovely day. Bitterly cold. To church twice & to Iron Room. Played for Service as Edith did not go! Walked home with Jane. Evelyn packed up. To bed late.

Morning Father. 2 Thessalonians III. 1-3

Afternoon Father 2 Thessalonians III. 1-3

Evening Father Acts IV. Mr Fenn could not come as he was hurt by a carriage yesterday coming from the station.

Monday 24th

Lovely day. V. cold. Up at 5 30. Father & Evelyn went off at 6 45. Emily & I churned 5 ¾ lbs. Up to the organ at 10 30. Edith stayed in for her cold. Emily & drove to Highgate in the carriage. Bitterly cold wind. Called in on the Maynards. Saw Miss Maynard & Gazy. Mr Fenn in bed. Began a small night school in hall – 8 came. Pleased & surprised. Had Reading & Writing.

With her father's love

Tuesday 25th

Lovely day. Went for a jolly ride at 11 15 to Benenden & back past Hole park. Left the books for M. Mitchell. In at 1 20. Rode the little horse. He went very well. To the village in the afternoon. To see Mrs Leney & Mrs Vaughan. Wrote to Charlie. Had the band of Hope for Girls. 14 there. Emily helped me – 2 new ones. Had Practice for men in the house – A. Burt came with Amos Catt.

Wednesday 26th

Fine day. Heard from & wrote to Evelyn & also to Dora. Sophie & Evelyn went to see the Jubilee presents with Charlie. Emily & I went up to Downgate. Mrs Hodgkin out but H showed us over the garden. Lovely chrysanthemums. Planted out some carnation cuttings. Edith had 25 at her Class. Maynard told her about George Shoebridge. Got encouragement.

Thursday 27th

Lovely early. Wrote to Mother. Had the horses at 10 15. Rode the big horse. He went <u>beautifully</u> by Newenden, Ewhurst, Northiam etc. Left a note at Mrs G. Piper's. Got in at 12 40. Had the Working Party. 9 came. To the Practice at 7. Good many. Tried some extra Choir hymns. B came in for cough mixture.

Friday 28th

Wet early. Cleared later. Much warmer. Had a nice letter from Arthur. Sent off my questions. Knitting a stocking on the machine. Walked into the village with Emily – to see Mrs Job Catt. Mrs A. Burt out. Mrs J.

Nash there. Then on in carriage with Edith. Called on Miss Cork & Miss Humphries – both out. To see Mrs Christmas & Mrs Robrancs. Had the boys for extra Practice. All 10 there. Enjoyed it v. much. George Shoebridge to see Edith. Very earnest. He signed the pledge.

Saturday 29th

Showery day. Up to the organ in the morning. Wrote the Choir papers etc. Helped Emily pack up in the afternoon. Then up to churchyard & put Forget me not all round our darling's grave. Emily & I went down to Old Place at 4 45. Jane had the 2nd Class Boys to tea. They all seemed very happy. Stayed about ½ an hour. Mr Chase arrived from Tunbridge Wells in the evening.

Sunday 30th

Wet early. Lovely later. Picked some violets for Eunice. Wrote to Evelyn. John Burt & John Smith came in to see me.

Morning I Girls only 6. Mr Chase Jeremiah XVIII. 2.

Afternoon Evelyn's boys to Mr Chase. Hebrews VI. 12. Played the organ in the afternoon.

Evening To the Iron Room. Mr Rising. Isaiah XXVIII.

Monday 31st

Lovely day. Emily & Mr Chase went off at 7 30. To the School at 10. Took the money. 36/7[76]. Got it all right. Wrote to Mother & Arthur. Sent A. a Hart's Tongue Fern. Mr Greenhill came to take the funeral of Burgis of Tenterden. He came in afternoon. Miss Thompson called with Mrs Burrows. Arranged the Mission Room. Had the Night School from 7 till 8 10. 19 came! Enjoyed it very much. Emily joined Sophie at Charlton.

NOVEMBER

Tuesday 1st

Showery day. Wrote to Pablo & to Margaret. Edith & I out at 12. Walked to Mrs G. Mallion's. Gave her the flannel petticoat. Then to Field Green to luncheon. Knitted in the afternoon. Very wet. Came home after tea. Had a Practice at the Mission Room at 7. 6 men & 4 boys came. Practised everything for the Service of Song. Prepared work for the Band of Hope.

Wednesday 2nd

Showery day. Hoped for a ride but too showery to get one. Wrote to Mother & Emily. To the village with Edith. I to see Mrs Judge, Mrs A. Burt & Mrs Taylor. Nice letter from Mother. Boys Band of Hope. 12. Edith had P.M. at 7 & Class at 7 30. 22. Jane to see me. Edith saw G.S. again.

Thursday 3rd

Very stormy day & rained heavily several times. Wrote to Kitty & Evelyn. Only 6 came to the Y.W.C.A. Miss Elsam & Miss Heaton stayed to tea. Walked down to Tan House. To the Practice at 7. Most of them there. Had a v. good Practice. Hymns, Psalms etc. Heard from Arthur & Evelyn.

Friday 4th

Stormy day again. Cox exercised the big horse. Down to the Lower End in the afternoon to see Mrs Bennett. Rained heavily so we hurried home. Heard from Leonard & wrote to him. Jane to tea with us. Her birthday. Gave her R.V. of Bible[77] with Edith. Night School. Only 5. George came up for reading. He told me all so seemed so bright & rejoicing.

Saturday 5th

Fine day. For a walk with Edith in the morning to see Mrs G. Mallion & Mrs R. Baines. <u>Better</u>. Miss Smith (Gramps) died. Heard from Arthur. Prepared lesson on Genesis XLV. Mr Chase arrived about 3 o'c. He told us much the same as last time. Worked in the evening. Very sleepy. To bed early.

Sunday 6th

Fine day. Joe Malcolm to tea. Nice talk & prayer with him.

Morning I Girls 10. Mr Chase Philemon 10. 11

Afternoon Evelyn's Class. 7. Mr Chase Luke XI. 42. Miss Elsam played in church.

Evening Mr Knight 2 Samuel IX. Mephibosheth again! Very solemn address.

Monday 7th

Showery day. Wrote to Mother. To the School in the morning for the money. 25/-. All right. Wet walk home. Told Mrs Taylor all about the Night School. Took Mrs Chase to the Maynards. On to the Cottage Hospital. Saw Mrs G. Mallion. Then to Lillesden for 2 hours. Night School in evening. 12 there. Brought Tom Barnes & Willie Burt.

Tuesday 8th

Fine day. Showery part of the day. Went for a splendid ride. 3 ¼ hours. By Benenden, Tenterden & Hole Park. Horses went beautifully. Enjoyed it very much. To the village in the afternoon to call on Miss Collins. Out. To Mrs Leney. Had the Girls Band of Hope. 16 there. Practice at Mission Room for Service of Song. Nearly all there. Played all the time. G.S. came up. Saw her.

Wednesday 9th

Very wet day. Heard from Mother & Emily. Wrote to Arthur, Emily, Evelyn & Leonard. Worked the knitting machine. Edith prepared a lesson on Jacob's Ladder[78]. She went to her class at 7 & had 26! Tom C. came in after. Very miserable. Jane to see me. Very nice hour together. Reading & prayer.

Thursday 10th

Fine day. To the organ in the morning. Edith found Tom bright & rejoicing. Praise God! Heard that Father & Mother come tonight. Working Party at 2 30 in the house. 9 there. Father & Mother arrived at 3 15. So nice to have them. Heard from Evelyn. To Practice at church – played most of the time.

Friday 11th

Showery day. To the organ in morning. For a drive in the brougham with Mother, Edith to Field Green. Saw them all. Left in the village to see Mrs Tester. Had the Boys to Practice at the Iron Room. Night School at 7. 19 again. Heard from Pablo.

Saturday 12th

Showery morning. Fine later. Up to the church in the morning. Wrote the Choir papers etc. Mr Vidler & another man to luncheon. Had a nice ride in the afternoon – by Field Green & the Junction. Very muddy but enjoyed it very much. George to see Edith to read etc. Mother made out part of a Co-op order. Heard from Pablo & Emma.

Sunday 13th

Lovely day but very dark & rainy! George Head came in to tea. He is out of work. Also, Durrant Booth. Heard from Leonard.

Morning   I Girls. 10. Communion – 42.

Afternoon   Evelyn's Class 10. Father. Hebrews XI. 23-24.

Evening   Mr Wallis. Hosea XIV 'Dew falls each night so Christ gives His Holy Spirit daily to those who ask Him'.

Monday 14th

Very wet morning. Cleared later. To the School for the money. Got it all right. Arranged the room for the evening. Got in at 2. Sophie came home & Eustace Hill with her. Helped Sophie unpack. To the Service of Song at 7 o'c. Room full! Evelyn & I sang 'Watered lilies'[79]. Mrs Taylor read 'Christie's Old Organ'[80] & the Choir sang.

Tuesday 15th

Lovely day. Very cold & a sharp frost. Edith & I walked to the village & round to Malt House with Eustace to see Mrs Mallion who has a bad foot. In the afternoon we 3 drove to Highgate to see the chrysanthemum show. Very good ones. I had the Night School at 7. 18 there. George S. & Tom came! They both stayed after for prayer with us. <u>So</u> nice.

Wednesday 16th

Fine, cold day. Edith & I walked to Field Green with Eustace. The D'A's were very kind. To see Mrs Blackwell. Mother began her Mothers' Meeting & had 16. To the village to see Mrs Catt, Mrs J. Smith, Mrs Booth & Mrs Field. Then to Iron Room. Jane to help me with the Band of Hope. 15 Boys. Father, Mother & Sophie dined at Lillesden. Edith had 17 at her Class. Played games.

Thursday 17th

Fine day. Still very cold. Eustace went away at 8 45. Not out in the morning. Helped Father do some Tithe calculations[81]. Had the Y.W.C.A. Class at 2 30. Not very many. Edith & I to the village after to see Mrs Judge & Mrs Lockyers. To the Practice with Sophie. Edith had George to see her. Willie Wickens signed the pledge.

Friday 18th

Showery day. Cox clipped both the horses. Watched him for some time. The little horse was fairly good. But he could not quite finish its head. Night School in the evening. <u>Very</u> wet & pitch dark. However, 12 came.

Saturday 19th

Fine day. Edith & I to the village. Took soup to Mrs Leney, Mrs Booth & Mrs Robbards & to see Mrs D. Catt. In the afternoon went for a jolly ride by Northiam & Ewhurst. Horses were very fresh & went most beautifully. It rained a little. We were out 2 ½ hours! Very quick. Saw Tom Clout in the evening. He signed the pledge! & I pinned on the little bit of blue[82].

Sunday 20th

Fine day. Willie Wickens came in to tea I & talked to him after. Found he could say 'My Saviour' & seemed so right. May he be a living witness! Praise God.

Morning   Father. Hebrews XII. 1-2.

Afternoon   Father. Hebrews XII. 1-2.

Evening   Mr Knight. Job VIII. 14. 'Spider'. 1st all web from within. 2nd can't raise itself – most striking. Miss Elsam & Miss Heaton came to tea & to the Evening Service.

Monday 21st

Fine day. To the School in the morning for the money. Got it all right. To see Mrs C. Willard. The others to the village. Down to Old Place & to see Mrs Moore, Mrs Catt & Jane. Nice talk with her. Mrs 'Adam' Catt buried. To the Night School. 18. Much improved. George & Tom stayed for prayers.

Tuesday 22nd

Fine day. Helped Father in the morning with some Tithe figures. Mother & Edith drove to Cranbrook. To the village to see Mrs Wickens, Mrs Moore, Mrs Mane, Mrs A. Field & Mrs Jeneford & to Girls Band of Hope. 22! 5 signed & 2 fresh ones. Practice for Young Men at 7. Began some new Church Choir – 3 girls.

Wednesday 23rd

Showery day. In all morning. Wrote to Charlie. To Downgate with Edith to see the chrysanthemums. Most lovely. Then round by the village to see Lizzie Mallion & Mrs R. Chantler. Mother had 18 at the Mothers' Meeting & Edith had 31! More than ever. She had P.M. after.

Thursday 24th

Fine day. Had a most jolly ride in the morning for 2 hours. By Junction & Cripps Corner. Horses went beautifully. Enjoyed it v. much. Edith to stay at the Maynards. Had the Working Party. 6 there. Sophie & Mother to Field Green. Wrote to Leonard. To the Practice with Sophie. Played part of the time.

Friday 25th

Lovely day. Wrote to Dora. Mother & Sophie to Rolvenden & Benenden. They drove me to the Lower End. To see Mrs Moore, Mrs J. Shoebridge,, Mrs Larkins, Mrs Christmas, Mrs Crisford, Mrs Chantler, Mrs Boye & old Mrs Catt. Then to the Lockyers & the Post Office. Sophie helped me at the Night School.

Had 20. Willie Wickens came. George came in to see me afterwards. Very nice talk & prayers with him.

Saturday 26th

Windy day. Heard from Lovedy & Mabel Carter. Worked the knitting machine. Made 1 pair & ½. Edith came back again. Round the shrubbery with her. Clara walked to the Tan House with me. Took some meat to Mrs C. Willard. Wrote the Choir papers etc. George to see Edith. He signed the pledge book & bought a coloured card.

Sunday 27th Advent Sunday[83]

Showery day. Had a nice talk with Willie after afternoon church. Mrs W. & George M. came to tea & walked down with us.

Morning Father.

Afternoon Father. Romans XIII. 10-11.

Evening Mr Weatherly. Titus II. 11-14. Very nice on Past, Present & Future.

Monday 28th

Fine day. To the School in the morning for the money & to see Mrs Leney after. For a jolly ride in the afternoon to Benenden & round by Rolvenden. Edith to the village & had the boys for Practice. Night School. 20. Alfred Shoebridge came.

Tuesday 29th

Fine day. Worked the knitting machine all morning. Made another pair of stockings. Drove to the village in the afternoon to see Mrs Judge & A. Burt. Had a Practice at the Mission Room – all came.

Wednesday 30th

Lovely day. Saw a most lovely star when we were called. Worked at some stockings in the morning. In the afternoon went ferreting with Cox & Tom! Got 3 rabbits. Then to the Mothers' Meeting Tea. 21 there. Changed several library books. Mrs Vaughan came in to see Mother. Edith had 27. Sophie took Class.

With her father's love

DECEMBER

Thursday 1ˢᵗ

Fine day. Walked to the village with Edith. Took soup to Mrs Leney & Mrs D. Catt. Stayed in & to the Y.W.C.A. Meeting with Edith. Jane <u>not</u> there! Lionel, Mabel & May came over & stayed to tea. They moved a verbena & a mryrtle. To the Practice with Sophie. <u>Very</u> few there.

Friday 2ⁿᵈ

Fine day. Down to Old Place in the morning. Took Mrs Moore some linsey[84] for a dress & to see Jane. Told her about yesterday. For a drive in the afternoon. Took Mrs Mallion to the Cottage Hospital. Then round by the Horns & home by Hawkhurst. Night School. 20.

Saturday 3ʳᵈ

Fine day. Prepared work etc & the room in the morning. Jane to help me at 2 30. Had 19 boys! 6 new ones. C. Burt, B. Clout, Henry Love! B. Hardy, W. Weller & Giles Small. Enjoyed having them very much. Prepared a lesson on the Word. Copied some more into my MS book.

Sunday 4ᵗʰ

Fine day. Had 1ˢᵗ Girls & II Boys again. After afternoon service John & Leonard Burt were baptised. Edith & I stayed & stood for them. A.B. & wife there too.

Morning Communion 53.

Afternoon Father. Romans XV. 3.

Evening Colonel Wisery. Luke XVII 'As it was in the days of Noah'. Miss Burgess & Miss Elsam to tea & Iron Room.

Monday 5th

Fine day. To the School in the morning & to see Mrs C. Willard. Father, Mother & Sophie to luncheon at Finchcox. In the afternoon walked across to see Mrs G. Mallion. Nice talk with her. Then to Mrs R. Chantler's & to the Iron Room. Boys came for practice at 4. Jane walked home with me. Night School. 25. Herbert Burt & G. Lockyer came to sign.

Tuesday 6th

Fine day. Not out much. To the Mission Room in the morning. Lay down in the afternoon. Heard from Leonard. Miss Legg sent me all my papers. Such a bundle! Practice at Mission Room. Nearly all there. Played all the time.

Wednesday 7th

Fine day. Began the Home Study papers. Walked to the village with Sophie. To see Mrs C. Willard & Mr Durrant – out. To the Mothers' Meeting Tea – 18. Edith to her class at the Iron Room & had 34! Wrote to Emily & Leonard.

Thursday 8th

Very wet day. Corrected Home Study all the morning. Father & Mother went away to join Emily & Evelyn in London. Only Jane & E. Bryant came. Practice in the hall. Not many. Began the anthem which went very fairly.

Friday 9th

Fine day. Corrected some papers. Arranged the Mission Room. Had the p. carriage. Cox drove. To see Mrs Simes, H. Stace, Mrs Lockyer, Mrs Booth & stayed some time with Miss Mimms who was still hoarse. Night School. 22. George Penfold came. Prayer with George & Tom for Monday. Father to Cambridge.

Saturday 10th

Snowy day. Finished correcting the papers. To the Mission Room. Put away the Night School things. Copied some poetry. Had the Girls Band of Hope at 2 30. 14 came. Jane to help me. Father & Mother came home bringing some pretty things for Xmas. Made out the Home Study maths in the evening. To bed late. Heard from May.

Sunday 11th

Showery day. Sharp frost early. 11 o'c thawed & rained after. Edith began her class at school. 32.

Morning I Girls. 11. Father. Jude III.

Afternoon II Boys. Father. Jude 14-15

Evening 7 o'c. Father. Ephesians I. 1-3.

Monday 12th

Fine day. Wrote to May & Miss Legg & sent off my papers. To the School at 10. Got the money all right. Then to see Mrs Jempson & Mrs Booth. Took some flannel. To the village again in the afternoon to see Mrs Rand, A. Burt & old Philip Milton. Then to the Iron Room for the Boys' Practice. Had 10. Night School in evening. 18 & had a Temperance Meeting after. 3. Tom, G.L. & P.C.

Tuesday 13th

Wet day. Emily & Evelyn came home. Busy getting their rooms ready & helped them unpack later. Copied out several things for the Service of Song. Evelyn came down with me to a Practice at the Iron Room. Mostly there – very rough night. Bertie Simes there. Heard from Lovedy.

Wednesday 14th

Fine day. Busy arranging Xmas cards & presents all the morning. Cloudy in the afternoon so we tidied our room. Went out to help at the Mothers' Meeting Tea. 17. Then put the room ready for the Bible Class which Sophie took as Edith's cold was very bad. 17. Heard from Dora.

Thursday 15th

Fine day. Very cold. In the garden in the morning. Evelyn for a ride at 2 o'c. I stayed in for the Y.W.C.A. Bible Class. Very nice. Edith talked about the 2nd Coming[85]. Discussed it with Miss Elsam. Sophie & Evelyn to the Practice! Sorry to miss it but my cold rather bad.

Friday 16th

Fine day. Heard from Pablo. Evelyn & I walked to the village. To Mrs Wood & Mrs Rains & round to Field Green. Saw Mrs D'A & Mabel. All busy preparing for Lionel's departure. Mrs Rollings bought 22/-[86] worth of things. Night School. Evelyn came out with me. 21.

With her father's love

Saturday 17th

Fine day. Went for a nice ride at 11 by village & Rolvenden. Enjoyed it very much. Had the Boys Band of Hope at 2 30. Evelyn helped me. 12 came. She told me about Dr Ink! Kept the Choir Boys for practice after. Then up to church with Evelyn. Pumped the organ for her for a few minutes.

Sunday 18th

Fine day. Edith had 27 at her Class. It rained hard part of the time going to the Iron Room.

Morning Father. I Girls

Afternoon Father. II Boys.

Evening Father. Ephesians I. 4-7.

Lionel came in to say 'goodbye'.

Monday 19th

Fine day. Went to the School with Emily. Took the money. Then to see Mrs Rand. Took a book to the children & to Mrs Wood. Lent a musical box & some marbles to Teddy. Down to Old Place in the afternoon. Nice time with Jane. Night School. 25. Had the Temperance Meeting after. 13! 7 new ones. Tom Barnes & 6 signed. James Webb, P. Weller, J. Bootle, G. Austen, Harry Stace & Herbert Smith.

Tuesday 20th

Fine day. Wrote a long letter to Lovedy. Sent her a little Calvary[87] for her birthday. To the village with Emily & Edith. To see Mrs Judge. Took her a Xmas packet & Mrs Wickens. Nice talk with her. Had the Scripture

Union Meeting at the Mission Room at 6. 38 children. Practice after. All there. They sang the carols etc nicely.

Wednesday 21st

Wrote several Xmas letters to Sarah, Frances Catt, Emma etc. Sophie & Evelyn walked to Field Green. Went to help at the end of the Mothers' Meeting. 18 there. Mrs Mills & Mrs Edmonds new ones. Leonard came home by Express & Charlie by the late train. Walked to the village to the Post Office & to Illmotts. Edith to the Iron Room. 27.

Thursday 22nd

Very cold day. Helped Leonard unpack. Wrote some more letters & sent off several cards. Had one from Miss Hesse. Only Mrs Field & Jane came to the Working Party. Read 'Children of the New Forest'[88] to them & Clara. Sophie & Evelyn to the Practice. Played 'Regina'. Gave a card with Isaiah XLV. 23 to A. Burt.

Friday 23rd

Fine day. Arranged the Mission Room. Then weighed out 16lbs of tea in 1lbs & ½ lbs & did them up. Cox drove Evelyn & me to the Lower End. Took tea to several. To see Mrs Robbards (G. Cocks), Ballow, Boys, Celia Vaughan, Verrall etc. Night School. 16. Evelyn & I took it & Sophie came to give out about payment. George came in after. Gave him a pair of cuffs.

With her father's love

Saturday 24th Christmas Eve

Fine day. Down to Old Place. Jane had a bad cold. Decorating at the church till 2 30. Then did up my presents. We gave them in the drawing-room after dinner. All very nice things. Arthur & May had their Xmas dinner tonight & dine with the Hoares on Monday. Played my new dominoes & 'Regina' later. To bed late. Had some more pretty cards & letters from Miss Douglas & Emma.

Sunday 25th Christmas Day

Lovely day. To church twice. Gave cards to both my Classes. Nice talk with Willie carter after church. Gave him his cards. Harry cut his knee on Friday. Sat with the children in the afternoon.

Morning Communion. 42. Piper & his wife, Penfold & Mrs R. Burt there. 1st Girls. Burt came into the Choir.

Afternoon II Boys. Father. Luke II.

Evening Father. Not many at Iron Room. Edith had 23.

Monday 26th Boxing Day

Fine day. Bitterly cold. It snowed a little. Had some more cards & a letter from Lovedy. Walked to the village with Charlie, Edith & Evelyn to post the letters. To see Mrs Wickens – out. Had our Christmas dinner in the evening. Played Nat. Hist. Dominoes with the servants.

Tuesday 27th

Heavy fall of snow in night. Edith & I plodded to village in morning. Arranged the room. Mr Jempson lent his harmonium. Stayed in all the afternoon. Miss Elsam to tea. Had the Service of Song at 7. 100 people. Mr Jempson & Miss Elsam sang solos & the Choir sang carols. Father read a Xmas story.

Wednesday 28th

Fine day. Freezing hard. Edith & I walked to the village in the morning to see Harry Wickens. Took him a book. Then to see Mrs Wood. Teddy better. To the Iron Room. To the village with Emily in afternoon. To see Mrs Job Catt, Mrs Simmonds, Booth, Leney & A. Field. Took Almanacs to them all. Heard from May & Mary Brazier. Mothers' Meeting put off. Edith's Class. 18.

Thursday 29th

Fine day. Went out ferreting with Charlie & Leonard. They got 8 rabbits. Very cold. To the Y.W.C.A. Class with Edith. Only 4 so did not go long. Then walked to the village to see Mrs Moore, Mrs Wickens. Took H. some bricks & my musical box. So pleased to see Mrs R. Barnes. Home with Emily. To the Practice in the evening at the Mission Room. Not v. many. Practised Psalms & hymns.

Friday 30th

Nothing recorded.

Saturday 31st

Nothing recorded.

NOTES

1. It had long been the custom, especially in the countryside, for bonfires to be lit on Twelfth Night bringing an end to the Christmas festivities.
2. The Feast of the Epiphany is an important Church Festival which is celebrated on 6th January. It recalls the visit of the Wise Men to the infant Jesus with their gifts of gold, frankincence and myrhh and the revelation of Jesus as divine. At the time of Mabel's diary, worship at St Nicholas would have centred on the use of the Book of Common Prayer (1662) in which some 6 Sundays are given as being 'after the Epiphany' and have their own Collects (Prayers) and Scripture readings, thus emphasising the importance of the whole of Epiphanytide.
3. Possibly 19, Upper Montague Street in Marylebone, London as this generally relates to other locations recorded in the diary.
4. The Young Women's Christian Association was founded in 1855 by Lady Mary Jane Kinnaird. It grew and soon spread around the world. The YWCA motto is from Zechariah 4: 6 'Not by might nor by power, but by my Spirit, says the Lord Almighty'. Today, it continues its work for the empowerment and rights of women in more than 100 countries. It would have had much appeal for the young Mabel.
5. 'Now the day is over', by The Reverend Sabine Baring – Gould, was a popular hymn since its introduction in 1865. Baring – Gould also wrote

another favourite hymn of the times, 'Onward Christian soldiers' (1865).

6. The Magnificat, also known as the Song of Mary, is based on the words spoken by Mary at the Visitation with her cousin, Elizabeth, which is described in Luke 1: 46 – 55. It has long been part of the worship of the Church. In the Church of England it is part of Evening Prayer (Evensong). It may have a variety of musical settings. The Psalms have been widely used in worship since the earliest of times. In the Church of England they are used in both Morning Prayer (Matins) and Evening Prayer.

7. The novel, 'John Halifax, Gentleman', was written by Dinah Craik in 1856.

8. 'Wives and Daughters, An every-Day Story' was written by Elizabeth Gaskell and first published as a serial in the Cornhill Magazine from 1864 – 1866.

9. 'Lean Hard' by Octavius Winslow, 'Just as I am' (1835) by Charlotte Elliott and 'There is a blessed home' (1861) by H.W. Baker.

10. The 14th Century moated castle at Bodiam is only 2 miles from Sandhurst.

11. Francis (Fanny) Crosby wrote 'Safe in the arms of Jesus' (1868). Amongst Crosby's many other hymns are such classics as 'Blessed Assurance (1873) and 'To God be the glory (1875).

12. The use of the traction engine in agriculture was only developed in the late 1850's so to find one in the parish was worthy of Mabel's exclamation.

With her father's love

13. Sandhurst is only 15 miles from Hastings to the South and 60 miles from London to the North West.
14. The story of Rahab is in Joshua 2: 1 – 24 where she is described as a one time prostitute living in Jericho who aided the Israelites in their capture of the city.
15. The Te Deum is a 4th Century hymn used widely throughout the Church. In the Church of England it forms part of Morning Prayer.
16. Almanacs were popular in Victorian Britain. They were published annually supplying much useful information on a variety of topics such as the weather, agriculture, weights & measures, the law and education as well as Church festivals. Almanacs often formed part of a diary such as that used by Mabel.
17. Possibly the workshops of James Chapman Bishop who established a premise at 250, Marylebone Road at the end of the 18th Century. The use of organs to accompany worship in church was hugely popular among the Victorians. No doubt as a keen organist Mabel would be most interested.
18. 16/6 would be expressed today as almost 83p. When inflation is taken into account its value would now be more than £100.
19. Princess Beatrice, 1857 – 1944, was the youngest of Victoria and Albert's children. She married Prince Henry of Battenburg, 1858 – 1896, in 1885.
20. Inflation would mean a value today of just over £900.

21. 30/- would be expressed today as £1.50. Inflation would mean that the cost would be around £190.
22. The Society for Promoting Christian Knowledge had been founded in the late 17th Century by The Reverend Thomas Bray. It worked to establish Christian schools and publish Christian literature so to develop the mission of the Church of England.
23. The Army & Navy Co-operative Society was founded in 1871 by service officers to offer goods to members at a beneficial rate. The premises in Victoria Street were popular among Victorian shoppers.
24. The Tabernacle was believed by the Jews to be the dwelling place of God. It was carried by them from the time of the Exodus until the conquest of Canaan. After the building of the Temple in Jerusalem it became superseded.
25. Quite what Mabel made of this is a matter of some conjecture.
26. Josiah Spiers began his work with children in 1867. It soon developed to become the Children's Special Service Mission, later becoming the Scripture Union.
27. Palm Sunday marks the beginning of Holy Week in the Church. On this day Christians recall the Triumphant Entry of Jesus into Jerusalem. Later in that week comes Maundy Thursday when Christians commemorate Jesus' betrayal, arrest and trials. The following day is Good Friday which, the day on which Jesus was crucified, is the most solemn day of the year in church.

With her father's love

28. The Brompton Oratory had only been completed in 1884. The church of the Congregation of the Oratory of St Philip Neri was dedicated to the Immaculate Heart of Mary. It is the second largest Roman Catholic church in London.
29. The Kent Ditch is a branch of the River Rother and runs locally between the parishes of Sandhurst and Bodiam.
30. Easter Day is the most important of all Church festivals when Christians celebrate their belief in Jesus' resurrection from the dead.
31. On this Bank Holiday Monday more than 100,000 demonstrators marched through London in protest of the government's response to the continuing so-called 'Irish Question' and also against a background of ongoing economic depression. Later in the year, on 13th November, matters came to a head when around 30,000 people had gathered in Trafalgar Square to protest a further time where they were met by some 2000 police and 400 armed troops, including cavalry. In the ensuing violence 400 demonstrators were arrested and 75 badly injured in what became known as 'Bloody Sunday'.
32. In the Church of England there is an annual Spring meeting of parishioners to elect churchwardens for the year.
33. Primrose Day is the anniversary of the death of the statesman and prime minister, Benjamin Disraeli, in 1881. He much liked the primrose and would often receive them from Queen Victoria. At

his funeral the Queen sent a wreath of primroses with the simple message 'His favourite flowers'.
34. Presumably, Mabel refers here to an embroidered sampler.
35. The Victorians had a passion for ferns and all things fern like. In the age of the amateur naturalist ferns were widely collected and cultivated. The fern motif was also used in many areas of art and design, and even appearing on the custard cream biscuit where it remains until today.
36. Inflation would mean a value of almost £260.
37. The Lent Lily is a wild form of the daffodil. Its name reflects that it often blooms and fades within the Church season of Lent in the Spring.
38. Launched in 1765 HMS Victory had seen service in the American War of Independence, the French Revolutionary Wars and the Napoleonic War. It was at the Battle of Trafalgar in 1805 that HMS Victory gained lasting fame as the flagship of Vice Admiral Nelson in Britain's naval triumph over the French and Spanish fleets. HMS Duke of Wellington was an early steam engine powered ship. By 1887 she had replaced HMS Victory as flagship of the Port Admiral at Portsmouth and would fire gun salutes for passing dignitaries.
39. The Channel Squadron was used by the Royal Navy to defend the English Channel.
40. Launched in 1863, HMS Minotaur was a 36 gun armoured iron frigate and the flagship of the Channel Squadron. HMS Monarch was an ironclad masted ship and the first in the Navy to have her guns in turrets. HMS Sultan was

With her father's love

launched in 1870 and also an ironclad ship. Her armament was carried in a central box battery.
41. As mass public education developed throughout the 19th Century the government used School Inspectors to examine schools and evaluate their success.
42. Ascension Day comes some 40 days after Easter and commemorates the Christian belief in Jesus' bodily ascension into heaven Mark 16: 19
43. 'I heard the voice of Jesus say "Come unto me and rest"' was written by Horatius Bonar in 1846 and was widely used at funerals.
44. 'Our own darling' is presumably a reference to Mabel's brother, John, who died in 1881 at the age of 26.
45. Whit Sunday (Pentecost) is a major Church festival. It is on the 7th Sunday after Easter when Christians celebrate the sending of the Holy Spirit to the first Christians as recorded in Luke 2: 1-11.
46. In the Church of England's Book of Common Prayer both the Monday and Tuesday following Whit Sunday are considered important and have their own Collect (Prayer) and scripture readings. Whit Monday had been a public Bank Holiday since 1871.
47. Turk and Jock were the family pet dogs. On a spare page at the front of her diary Mabel records the weights of the two dogs together with those for the rest of her family. Turk is 4st. (25kgs) while Jock weighs 1st. 8lbs (9.5 kgs).
48. Trinity Sunday comes on the Sunday after Whit Sunday and celebrates the Christian belief that God is a Trinity of Three Persons – Father, Son

and Holy Spirit. In the Book of Common Prayer there are then 25 Sundays known as 'Sundays after Trinity' until the end of the Church year.

49. The Lambeth Conference is an assembly of bishops from the worldwide Anglican Communion which gathers every 10 years. Interestingly, the Third Lambeth Conference did not assemble until the next year, 1888, so perhaps Mabel's father was involved in some aspect of its forward planning.
50. This would be expressed today as 25p. Inflation would mean a value now of more than £32.
51. The 19th Century was a period in which the Church of England engaged in much missionary work, especially in the overseas colonies. Mabel was a keen supporter of such work.
52. Queen Victoria's Golden Jubilee was celebrated on 20th June 1887. The following day there was a service to mark the occasion at Westminster Abbey.
53. Mildmay was one of the most important home and overseas missionary organisations in the country at this time. It also did much to advance the position of women. It was through Mildmay that the role of Deaconess was introduced by which young women were trained and tasked for work in the Church often in poor areas where they provided much needed medical assistance. Mildmay continues its work of caring today especially in the area of HIV and AIDS, both in this country and abroad.
54. 107 Fahrenheit is around 42 Celsius.

With her father's love

55. 'The Pilgrim's Progress' was written by John Bunyan in 1678. It is a classic of English spiritual writing.
56. In the Book of Common Prayer there is a prayer 'For Rain' and also one 'For Fair Weather'.
57. Christians believe that it is important to share their faith with those around them. This quote comes from Mark 5: 19 'But Jesus refused, and said to him, 'Go home to your friends, and tell them how much the Lord has done for you, and what mercy he has shown you."
58. Typhoid was a major contributor to the death rate in Victorian Britain. It is usually caused by drinking water which has been contaminated with sewerage. Typhoid was an endemic problem associated with the squalid living conditions of the urban poor. There were typhoid epidemics in the early part of Victoria's reign.
59. By this Mabel will have meant that Burt was unable to accept Jesus Christ as his personal Saviour. An emphasis on the importance of personal experience of faith was a developing theme in the Victorian Church.
60. 'Preston Fight' written by William Ainsworth in 1875 was an historical novel set in the Jacobite Risings of the early 18th Century.
61. A glee is a popular type of English song scored for at least 3 voices and often sung unaccompanied.
62. The application of a linseed poultice to the chest and back was a long standing treatment of pleurisy.

63. The effects on the health of those ex patriots who lived and worked in the Far Eastern colonies were widely acknowledged.
64. 'Burmah' is the old spelling of 'Burma' which today is known as Myanmar.
65. 'Squails' was a table top game in which participants hit discs with the heel or palm of the hand aimed at a jack.
66. 'Daily Light' was a devotional book of Biblical readings and accompanying spiritual reflections arranged around themes. It was hugely popular in Victorian Britain. First published in 1875 it has continued ever since.
67. 'The voice that Breathed o'er Eden' (1857) by John Keble and 'How welcome was the call' (1861) by H.W. Baker.
68. On 16th September 1887 there was a terrible rail accident at Hexthorpe, two miles from Doncaster. An excursion train carrying almost 1000 passengers was run into by a Liverpool to Hull train. 25 were killed and 94 were badly injured.
69. The recent Anglo-Egyptian War of 1882 in which Britain established an influence in the country prompted much interest at home.
70. From Joel 2: 21.
71. 'Cranford' was written by Elizabeth Gaskell. It was published between December 1851 and May 1853, in the magazine 'Household Words'.
72. 26 degrees Fahrenheit is around -3 degrees Celsius.
73. The Church of England had long held a concern for the pastoral care and spiritual welfare of seamen. During the 19th Century a number of

With her father's love

organisations involved in the area emerged. In 1856 it was decided that that there should be an umbrella organisation called 'The Mission to Seamen, Afloat, at Home and Abroad'. Two years later the name was changed to 'The Mission to Seamen'. In 2000 the name changed again to 'The Mission to Seafarers' which now cares for all who work on the seas irrespective of race, nationality, rank or gender.

74. Mabel's 21st birthday. A very significant date as this was her age of majority. It was not until 1970 that the age was further reduced to 18.
75. Inflation would mean a value now of £6, 450.
76. This would be expressed today as £1.83 and inflation would mean a value now of £236.
77. The 'Revised Version of the Bible' is the only authorised and recognised revision of the King James Bible in Britain. The New Testament was published in 1881 and the Old Testament 4 years later.
78. A reference to the story of Jacob in Genesis 28: 10-19 in which he dreamed that he saw a ladder going from earth to heaven with angels ascending and descending on it.
79. Probably based on the Christian poem of the same name.
80. 'Christie's Old Organ, Or, "Home Sweet Home"' was written by Mrs O.F. Walton and published by the Religious Tract Society in 1874. It tells the story of the orphan Christie and how he found a home and faith.
81. Tithes were a tax which required 1/10th of all agricultural produce to be paid annually to the

local church and clergy. Payment was expected irrespective of whether a person attended the church for worship.

82. The Temperance Movement had arisen as a reaction to widespread drunkenness which was prevalent in 19th Century Britain. It received much support from the Church. Mabel makes several references to Temperance and was involved in the Band of Hope whose, members had to pledge to abstain from all intoxicants, except as a medicine. In the early 1880's the cause of Temperance was revived from America by the Gospel Temperance or Blue Ribbon Movement. The blue ribbon badge became widely recognised as a symbol of a person having taken the pledge to abstain. It is based on Numbers 15: 38-39 'Speak to the Israelites, and tell them to make fringes on the corners of their garments throughout their generations and to put a blue cord on the fringe at each corner. You have the fringe so that, when you see it, you will remember all the commandments of the LORD and do them, and not follow the lust of your own heart and your own eyes.'

83. Advent is a season in the Church calendar which goes on for the period of time marked by the 4 Sundays before Christmas Day and is a time of great expectation, waiting and anticipation. In the Book of Common Prayer each of these Sundays has its own Collect and Scripture reading. Advent Sunday marks the beginning of the Church year.

84. Linsey (Linsey-Woolsey) is a plain woven fabric which has been in use since ancient times.

With her father's love

Because it was made from both wool and linen its use was prohibited for the Jews in the Torah (Law) – Leviticus 19: 19 'Do not wear clothing woven of two kinds of material'.

85. Christians believe that Christ's First Coming was as a baby born in Bethlehem and his Second Coming will be at the end of time when he will return to judge all people. It is an important theme in the season of Advent – the 4 Sundays before Christmas.
86. 22/- would be expressed today as £1.10. Inflation would put its value now as around £140.
87. In essence, a small model depicting the crucifixion of Jesus.
88. A children's novel written by Frederick Marryat in 1874. It is set in the time of the English Civil War.

ABOUT THE AUTHOR

Stephen Huggins is a priest in retirement who lives in East Sussex with his wife, Toni and their daughter, Ruth.

Printed in Poland
by Amazon Fulfillment
Poland Sp. z o.o., Wrocław